Dream Merchants
& HowBoys

Dream Merchants
& HowBoys

Mavericks, Nutters and the Road
to Business Success

BARRY J. GIBBONS

CAPSTONE

First published 2002 by
Capstone Publishing (a Wiley company)
8 Newtec Place
Magdalen Road
Oxford OX4 1RE
United Kingdom
http://www.capstone.co.uk

British Library Cataloguing in Publication Data
A CIP catalogue record for this book is available from the British Library.

ISBN 1-84112-186-X

Typeset in 11/16 pt Palatino by
Sparks Computer Solutions Ltd, Oxford
http://www.sparks.co.uk
Printed and bound by
T.J. International Ltd, Padstow, Cornwall

This book is printed on acid-free paper

Substantial discounts on bulk quantities of Capstone books are available to corporations, professional associations and other organisations. For details telephone Capstone Publishing on (+44-1865-798623), fax (+44-1865-240941) or email (info@wiley-capstone.co.uk).

IN MEMORY OF MY DAD

DREAM MERCHANT EXTRAORDINARY

Contents

Prologue

Learn a little,
Laugh a little,
Steal a lot

S INCE I LEFT CORPORATE LIFE and, more recently, returned to live in England after a decade or so in the USA, I have run my private business affairs as a tight ship.

Nonetheless, as my team assembled for our weekly Strategy and Mission Statement review, it was difficult to get them all around the big oak table in the Stone Jug pub in the village of Clophill, Bedfordshire. As they arrived, and manoeuvred for position to be near me, I ticked them off against my mental register.

First, there were my lawyers – a dozen of them neatly arranged in two rows, taking up the whole of one side of the table. My accountants and bankers also grouped together, for reasons best known to themselves, and clustered, untidily, at one end. Opposite me, in no particular order, sat my two chauffeurs (the other being on vacation), my masseuse, my pilot, my chef and my personal *barista*. Squeezed on the corner was the chappie who catalogues and organises my cufflinks. He was also covering for the guy who does my neckties. My head of IT and Communications busied herself with the video conferencing link to my US team, which numbered about the same, and who were all assembled around the family table in Los Gallegos tapas bar in Miami.

We were all set to begin, having left two empty chairs. The first of these was for Prince Edward, who had agreed to attend on a *pro bono* basis to help us with some complicated accounting issues concerning business losses. The second, permanently empty these days but left there as a mark of respect, was for Jeffery Archer, who used to be an enormous help with my diary planning.

I nodded twice, almost imperceptibly, to the waiting bar staff – which they knew to be a sign to deliver the first two courses (oysters and Black Velvet, followed by mockingbird foreskins *farcie*) in exactly half an hour from the first of the two nods – and called the meeting to order.

As usual, I asked for agenda items. After a l-o-n-g minute's silence (isn't it funny how no one likes to be first?), one of the lawyers mumbled something. With a lot more grace and sensitivity than I felt, I told him not to be nervous, and asked him – in a kindly way, I think – to speak up a bit. His contribution stunned us all:

'We are due to produce another book. It says here by the end of August.'

My first thoughts were repetitive, along the lines of 'Shit-Shit-SHIT'. That was not what I articulated of course. I was calmness personified:

'Absolutely so. I have every faith in us all to rally round and produce a winner within the time constraints involved. Anybody got any early ideas?'

A shuffling sound came from an adjacent table, where my panel of private secretaries sat (I forgot to mention them in my introduction). It was, I think, Fifi who spoke up:

'Given the sales of the last one, perhaps we could goose the whole thing up a little? I'm thinking of a title along the lines of *Harry Potter and Seven Points for an Effective Business Strategy*.'

Silly woman. Still, fresh from a recent Diversity Workshop, I remembered my newly-learned mantra – that one should not respond to suggestions made in an open forum, which contained a population of anything other than cranky, middle-aged white males, with the words: 'I support *but* ...' The correct response is, of course, 'I support *and* ...' – which is non-threatening, positive and inclusive. (Snore, groan, fart.)

So, I built on her idea. Sort of. You could have heard a pin drop as I began to share my exciting concept:

'I want you all to think back to the time when ABBA quit as a wildly successful pop group. In particular, I want you all to focus your minds on the dark-haired bird. She's the one who could sing and didn't have a beard. When the band broke up, she disappeared from sight – completely. Am I correct?'

Many of them had their eyes closed by now, in deep concentration. Brows were furrowed, and a couple of the lawyers were deep in a whispered argument. I seized the moment and carried on:

'Now then, am I also correct in my theory that, just as she disappeared, Anita Roddick burst on the scene with Body Shop?'

I ignored the gasps and ploughed on:

Tell me if I am wrong – but isn't it an indisputable fact that, from that day onwards, those two have never been seen together and never been photographed together?'

I paused for dramatic effect:

'The dark haired bird from ABBA and Anita Roddick, are, ladies and gentlemen, without doubt *one and the same person.*'

I gave them no chance to digest this before hitting them with the Big Idea:

'And, what is more, there are others out there. Major business leaders, who are really somebody else. There is our book.'

The silence was, in its own way, stunning. It was broken with a strangled cry from my masseuse:

'Jesus, you are right. I've always thought Walt Disney was really Bing Crosby and, do you know, they were also never photographed together.'

I forgave her the small blasphemy as she was caught up in the swell of excitement. Suddenly bedlam took over. Prince Edward took his seat, and *nobody noticed.* A lawyer leapt to his feet and pounded the table:

'That Branson guy – you know, him with the beard? Well, let me tell you, he *didn't used to have one.* That's because he used to be in the Beach Boys, *but they killed him off.*'

With difficulty, I brought the meeting to order, but not before learning who Steve Jobs of Apple really used to be, which was astonishing. It was time to bring order out of chaos, and assert my legendary leadership:

'Calm down, calm down. Yes, we have something unique here, but we must be careful. We are required to provide a business book, not some cheap sensationalism. We will analyse all these business leaders who used to be somebody else, but dress it up in a way that gets it on the six hundred linear miles of shelving dedicated to business books that is now a feature of all bookstores. I have, naturally, some ideas ...'

There was a scurrying and shuffling as they all scrambled for their pens and jotters to take notes. I counted to ten, then carried on:

'First, we need the book to be informative. Folk need to learn useful *snippets* about our heroes and their businesses, so that they can impress their bosses at work and/or members of the opposite (or their preferred) sex in bars. This will not be one of those regurgitated summary biographies of a bakers' dozen of assorted business leaders, but it will be informative. Disney, as only they can, have invented a word for this kind of thing – *infotainment.*'

A lot of them were having trouble spelling that last word, and at least one threw up at the whole idea. I was, however, merciless now, and ploughed on:

'The second thing we need in this book is some *humour.* Everything about business today is grey and humourless. Everybody is stressed, pressured and paranoid. The whole business world is populated by miserable bastards. Smiling is going the way of smoking – soon it will only be allowed outside on the street at coffee break time. The people we have listed were (or are) anti-grey. Whether we love them or hate them, they are colourful. So, while we are figuring them out, we must allow for a few grins.'

The excitement had become too much for Chanteuse, my manicurist, who had arrived late and been swept along by the energy of the last few minutes. She passed out, but we just left her there, sprawled across the pool table. This was no time to stop the momentum, and all eyes were now on me, expectantly:

'Finally, and of primary importance, we must use the experience of these inspiring people to give the ordinary folk in business some things that they can use, back in their own workplaces. Sure, these *Grandes Fromages* achieved successes on a scale that is way beyond the dreams of most people who roll up to the office each day – but, if we poke around, we will, I know, find ideas and ways of doing business from these people which can be transferred to the daily grind which faces most of us. Our dreams are more mundane, and our tasks less grandiose – but they still have to be done. I believe we can learn a ton of stuff from these people, which is *relevant to our lives.*'

I closed the meeting. There was an excited buzz in the air as the oysters arrived, but I was strangely silent. *Learn a bit, laugh a bit, steal a lot* – that was the challenge we had agreed for the book. We had rapidly established a list of names. If only I could now think of another way of linking these strange people together which would make sense for a business audience. The intriguing fact that they had all been somebody else was not enough; *there must be something else.*

Gradually, an idea formed. I opened my laptop and began to type.

Barry Gibbons,

Bedfordshire, England,

summer, 2001.

Email: Gibbonfile1@aol.com

Introduction

I   GENESIS

ANY PUBLISHED AUTHOR, with the possible exception of Jeffrey Archer, will tell you that writing a book is an exercise of love.[1] So this makes my motive in writing this book nothing exceptional. But I do love Nutters. Or, at least, those that fall in my definitive net.

I confess that my original working title for this book reflected that position. It was, simply, *Nutters*. As I progressed into the second minute of the project, however, it became clear that I probably needed

---

[1] In his case, it used to be an exercise in typing. Now, it involves a smuggled pencil.

---

to concentrate on selected sub-categories. Whereas I was quite clear what my definition included and excluded, there was a risk that the less informed reader might be mislead at the early, crucial, book-buying point. Where all of my Nutters have some positive attributes, and some of them little else, there was a risk that the all-encompassing title could link them, by association, with, for example, those Nutters who amble into America's schools and let fly with assault rifles.

It would not be over-fair to link some of the great names in this book as fellow-Nutters. Normally, this would not have bothered me too much. As I write, however, the George W. Bush presidency is gathering momentum, and only the brave would rule out capital punishment being introduced for libel. I needed to sub-categorise. As the Americans might say, I needed to acc-en-tuate the positive.

I would like you to join me on the short journey that ended with the Nutter sub-categorisation that became the main title of this book.

Nutters, in my definition, are the kind of folk that, when you see or hear of something they have done or said, you stare ahead for a while. Then, a faint smile begins to crinkle the corner of your mouth, and you ask yourself, quietly at first, just *what the hell were they think-, ing?* Were they MAD? Then, aloud, you laugh and sort of celebrate, actually with them and on their behalf.[2] Jealousy is in the mix of emotions somewhere. Absolute Nutterness, but the world was a better place as a result of it.

Sometimes, there is a next stage.

I have spent an alarming chunk of my life in Big Business, on both sides of the Atlantic. I suppose my own world highlighted Business Nutters. When I looked a little more closely at some examples, I not only laughed (see above) and questioned the sanity of the perpetrators – I celebrated and saw that the world was a better place post-Nutterness. I found remarkable evidence that some Nutterness works. Never mind the world at large, *the business itself benefited in*

---

[2] In an advanced case, you will laugh a laugh that causes you to lose control of some bodily functions and pass wind.

the short, medium or long term. Sometimes all of the above, and sometimes enormously so.

Out of boredom one day, I tried plotting them on a scattergraph. There were, in my observation, too many patterns and too many correlations for all the dots to be classed as random. While it was worth studying each dot in its own right, I began to dream of finding a way to join some of them up. A long time before I wrote these words, the genesis of this book was emerging from its own, rather strange, time-space continuum amidst the gently swaying palm trees of South Florida. They were only swaying gently because, at this specific time, we were outside the hurricane season.

In the beginning I was on a really ugly stretch of road. You may take my word for this. I was born in the industrial north of England and have driven through Oldham; I know what ugly roads look like.

Moving north towards the city of Miami, I was driving on South Dixie Highway, part of the US1 road system which stretches along the east coast of the Unites States from Canada to the Florida Keys. Although, for the serious long-distance driver it has been long superseded by parallel turnpikes and expressways, it is, I believe, still possible to drive its length – as it is for its more striking and romantic 'sister' road on the west coast, the Pacific Coast Highway.

It was at the beginning of the 1990s. The developed world was in a deep recession. I was not long into my time on the bridge of the good ship Burger King Corp. The ailing company had been acquired by the British company I worked for previously, GrandMet, in one of the last great contested acquisitions of the eighties. I had made the journey from Bedfordshire, England, to Miami, arguably Havana's northernmost suburb. I had been chairman and CEO of the company for less than two years.

The company had spent the last ten years achieving the corporate equivalent of peeing on its own shoes.[3] It was in a mess. On top of that, it was based in Miami. There is a strong case to put that if

---

[3] I have NO IDEA of the female equivalent of this analogy. Sorry.

God was giving the earth an enema, Miami would be among the top choices for the location of the hole in which to insert the tube. The general consensus of some of my friends, family, colleagues and peers was that I was a Bloody Nutter to take it on. The consensus among the rest of them was that I had a chance *because* I was a Bloody Nutter. It was, in fact, in their humble opinion, the only chance.

I was driving my company car. I was a heady combination of a new arrival in the US and a complete arsehole – so I had (naturally) chosen a Cadillac the size of a small cruise liner. As a small defence against my arseholeness, I was driving myself, having banned chauffeurs and limos as corporate symbols of why the company had gone wrong in the first place. In fairness, these examples of corporate indolence were but a small part of the mix that had resulted in Burger King, and its parent company Pillsbury, achieving the business equivalent of covering themselves with leaves and hibernating while their respective competitors ate their metaphoric lunch. In Burger King's specific case, this was added to by gems such as the $63 million cash purchase of a palatial purpose-built corporate headquarters, right on the ocean, about ten miles south of Miami. In time, this building proved to be a) completely unusable by anybody, or for anything, else and b) a prime target for the meandering but lethal Hurricane Andrew.

It was from this building that I, Captain Kirk, was heading north, in my Cadillac Starship, to the airport, via US1. I was far from happy.

Some brief background to explain why: Burger King is a franchised system – with less than ten percent of its (now) ten thousand or so restaurants owned and run by the company itself. This has huge implications for the business *modus operandi,* and the leadership thereof. The best way I have found to illustrate the difference to politely bored people, who show some interest, is to point out that Burger King does not sell burgers to burger-eaters – it sells franchises to businesses. It is *they* who then sell burgers to burger-eaters.

The main corporate product of a company like Burger King is a branded restaurant system. In our case it was developed over five decades. Our customers (aka franchisees) pay an upfront fee to buy that product. They then invest their own money in assets such as land, buildings and kitchen equipment to build a restaurant and operate that branded system. The franchisees then pay a continuing percentage of the sales revenues generated by these restaurants to the corporation. The hard, tangible assets that make up the restaurants and real estate appear on the franchisee's balance sheets, and the sum of such assets in a largely franchised system such as Burger King *often exceeds the total assets that the corporation has invested in the company*. Burger King might sell two or three franchises a day across the world. The Burger King franchisees, collectively, would sell two million Whoppers (burgers) a day.

If there is a better formula for a bigger Corporate Pissing Contest than that between franchisor and franchisee(s) in a big multinational, branded, franchised system on the whole of Planet Business, I am not aware of it. Leading it, as I was, as the corporate *Grande Fromage*, was like walking in a minefield. Before my spell, there had been either seven previous CEOs in thirteen years, or (more likely) thirteen CEOs in seven years. My secretary, who had lived through whichever combination it was, had lost track. Like I gave a toss.

The spirit of the franchisor/franchisee relationship is that the former owns the brand. It has absolute discretion over every aspect of the basic specification – from, in Burger King's case, sandwich recipes to server's uniforms. From broiler specification to ketchup supply. From point-of-sale posters to portion control. Everything. It maintains and develops all aspects of the brand. It markets it at macro level. It makes sure economies of scale are effectively and efficiently brought into play in purchasing and distribution. It is responsible for the overall IT system architecture. It ensures legal compliance. It governs where existing restaurants operate, and who operates them. It has papal approval over all new franchisees and locations. It polices franchisee performance, and should move to sanction underperforming or recalcitrant franchisees. It uses the incoming one-off fees and continuing royalty payments to fund all this and make a return for its investors.

Although it should only franchise a system if it is tried and trusted, it cannot and should not underwrite the independent *business* risks of any franchise that buys a system and/or any franchised location that operates it. The franchisees should accept all the above and quietly and efficiently deliver the defined brand to delighted customers – making a fortune for themselves in the process.

That's the spirit, the *theory*.

In reality, in the eyes of the franchisees, the corporate executives usually discharge these responsibilities like wankers. In the eyes of the franchisors, franchisees usually operate their precious brand like tossers. So there.

The leader sits firmly in the middle.

I was musing on the irony of this, and I still had – what? – about two miles to go before the billboard appeared. Of course, I didn't know that then.

In Burger King's case, both sides were right. GrandMet had paid a lot for the Pillsbury group, and I found out later our corporate masters had shoved[4] more than the fair share of the acquisition price Burger King's way in an attempt to make Pillsbury (which was what they *really* wanted) look good. As a brand-owning corporation, if we were to make the required investor returns, we didn't have enough financial headroom to spend what we wanted to spend to maintain and develop the brand. In truth, we didn't have enough to spend what we *should* have spent – in particular for the American franchisees.

Our challenge was complicated by the fact that the vast majority of our franchisees were in the US – in a maturing market and an under-invested and badly run state. It needed huge quantities of money to be invested by both sides. But we had bigger problems

---

[4] The technical expression for this is, of course, allocated.

internationally, where not one of our franchises was healthy. These, too, needed investment – in many cases just to buy them out and start again. Add to that the fact it was the international market where we saw our real growth potential – and each new market cost money to enter. When we spent a few hundred million US dollars to acquire the UK Wimpy locations, so that we could convert the cream of them to Burger King and give us a flying, 150-location start to a UK growth program, the US franchisees didn't see it as a synergistic expansion of the brand that would have benefits for all involved. They saw it as corporate investment that should have gone to the US to plug some holes and do some stuff.

Then there was our first US advertising campaign. As my musing mind opened this chapter, the billboard was still about a mile away.

We had a honeymoon period with our US franchisees. In fairness, their previous US 'masters' – a combination of corporate executives in Burger King, and more senior ones in the Pillsbury parent group, had run the brand so badly that they would have given Tiny Tim a chance. At the start, we did a lot of things that went down well. They had been starved of new ideas, new products and new attitudes – and we gave them enough to choke a medium-to-large sized python. A million changes. Some were welcomed, some not. But everybody was waiting for our first advertising campaign.

In 'Have It Your Way' Burger King had, in its archives from twenty years previously, one of the great, and greatly effective, advertising campaigns in the history of the science (or art – you choose). Since then, a major bone of contention from the franchisee community was that the advertising had been crap. The advertising is 'owned' by the franchisor, and developed by an outside marketing agency that is retained by them. The franchisees, via innumerable committees, have their say and input – but the papal sign-off belongs to the franchisor. This annoys the franchisees because they pay for the creative development and buying media – via another royalty contribution based on restaurant sales, which is then pooled for that specific purpose. It becomes dangerously near taxation without representation – especially if it doesn't work. 'Work' being defined here as hauling the sales graph upwards, quickly.

Burger King's immediate history, prior to our takeover, was of failed advertising campaigns. Sales refused to budge – other that in their gentle downward trend motion. Part of that is due – and here's a personal value judgement – to the fact they were creatively poor campaigns. But a more salient reason was that *no* campaign, anywhere, for anybody, was recording the high, fast, returns of the days of network television dominance. There were many more media channels to dilute the impact of any spend. The general branded market was immensely more cluttered than at any time in history. I read and digested figures at the time that indicated ordinary US consumers could be exposed to 3000 brand 'messages' a day from the moment they woke and switched on the radio, to the moment they went to bed with a magazine.[5]

Now, add to that the fact that our franchised restaurants had become less attractive and less unique. Hard times in this business sees the labour (aka service levels) cut, cosmetic maintenance delayed and prices often hiked. In addition, on every street, new, bright, competition was emerging – selling tacos or chicken or pizza. National advertising had long since stopped being a silver bullet, but that didn't stop our franchisees praying for one – and demanding that we deliver it.

We launched a campaign called 'Sometimes You Gotta Break The Rules'. It was aimed at rekindling our 'Have it Your Way' uniqueness. The 'rule' in fast food hamburgers – as exemplified by McDonalds – was that you didn't make individual sandwiches, you made a batch, and served the customer from that batch. We didn't, we made it when you ordered it. We could 'individualise' the order ('Hold the pickle'). That was the 'rule' we 'broke'. Clever, huh? A second industry rule was that you fried the burger in its own fat. We broke that

---

[5] I read somewhere that this figure is now, in 2001, a decade after these events, some THIRTY THOUSAND A DAY. I can't remember the source, but until somebody proves otherwise to me, I'm gong to assume it's true. It certainly seems that way.

rule, too – we broiled our burger patties. The fat went away. We positioned the creative element of the advertising to highlight that rule breaking, and show us as a bit mischievous – the kind of scruffy, loveable little boy in class, compared to the do-goodie, teacher's pet (aka McDonalds). I was delighted with it. Still am. Bloody Nutter.

When it hit the screens, very little happened. Nothing good, nothing bad. Essentially it proved a defensive spend – in line with our thinking that the only way we would get big growth again was to improve the offering in the restaurant, not on the TV screen.[6]

The franchisees, collectively, started a low grumbling noise. Then, I opened my mail one day and found a letter of complaint from a big US Parent/Teacher's Association – accusing us of encouraging children to become criminals (sometimes you gotta break the rules ... geddit?). This was copied to the press. It was shortly followed by the Teamsters Union, saying their members were under enough pressure to drive too fast and cut corners as it was – this was encouraging irresponsible truck driving. Then, The Campaign For A Drug Free America wrote in – copy to *USA Today* – did I realise just *what* I was encouraging? ... Then about fifty more, all copied to the press. Then the press came at us. The franchisees' quiet grumble became a roar. At a stroke, they turned their guns away from the competitive enemy, and pointed them all back at the general's tent.

It was then I realised that, at the birth of the US nation, some two hundred years before, along with the articulation of the timeless Constitution, somebody had taken the fledgling nation to one side and surgically removed its fucking sense of humour. Fat lot of good that realisation did me.

I was deep in thought as to how the hell you could do anything to grow the system, against a background of a relationship between franchisor and franchisee that seemed to be based on zero trust, zero respect, underinvestment and poor performance on both sides. That was when I saw the billboard.

---

[6] Which eventually proved to be the case.

It was the first time I had seen it. Many of you will remember it now. I will never forget it. In stark colour and highlight, it was a blow-up photograph of a woman's figure. Whether she was standing or sitting wasn't clear – the image was cut off above the neck and below the rib cage. She was effectively naked. She was clearly of African birth or descent. The skin was a rich, dark, chocolate colour. The three main colours of the image, the woman's body, the apricot-coloured blouse opened and pushed back and to the side, and the plain pastel background, were offset by the darker shade of an exposed nipple. If there is a shade called 'dark chocolate with a hint of lavender', this nipple was of it. Only one nipple was exposed. The other was hidden from view, suckling, as it was, a tiny white-pink baby. The contrast of skin colour hit you like a sledgehammer. The fusion of their activity dropped your jaw. On the top right of this billboard sized image was the only writing. In capital letters it said: UNITED COLOURS OF BENETTON.

The imagery was staggering. It was beautiful, evocative, erotic, stunning, heart-warming and simple. All at once. Clearly, it was political dynamite. If ever a picture spoke a million words, this was it. Right by the billboard site, one of Miami's most popular suburban seafood restaurants plied its trade. In the eleven years I have known it, it has never had an African-American waiter or waitress.

The billboard had gone two days later.

At that stage, I knew nothing of Toscani (the photographer used). I knew little about the shadowy Luciano Benetton. I did know that Benetton were a franchise-type system,[7] I presumed they enjoyed the same kind of relationship with their franchisees that we did (i.e. delicate, to say the least). I knew they were trying to grow in the US, and having difficulty. I knew that they were about the same size as Burger King across the world.

---

[7] Benetton operate a different model with their store owners. The latter are independent business people, but it is not a franchise in the US sense of the word. See later.

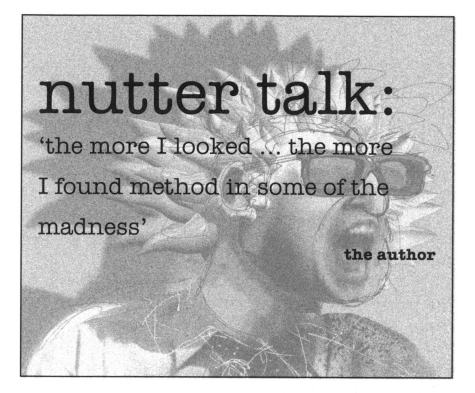

nutter talk:

'the more I looked ... the more I found method in some of the madness'

the author

The image stayed with me. I didn't know whether to be thrilled by somebody taking this kind of edgy, in-your-face brand positioning, or aghast. I ended up both. Two words kept circling my head for the rest of my journey.

Bloody Nutter.

It was around then that I started to develop my fascination for Nutters. The more I became fascinated, the more I looked into Nutterness. And vice-versa.

Then something started to come out of the other end. The more I looked, and the more I became fascinated, the more I found method in some of the madness.

II GENESIS TOO

I began (mentally) to collect examples of Nutterness, partly out of self-interest. Here's why: by the start of the nineties I had been in big business, at increasingly senior levels, for over twenty years. The pace of my progress through the ranks, from a graduate entry with Shell in the UK in 1967, to a US-based chairman and CEO of one the world's largest, branded restaurant systems in 1989 had been startling. I once calculated that my average tenure in a job had been less than eighteen months. Invariably, I had been promoted and/or the job had doubled in size and/or headhunters had called and whisked me away.

It had been exhilarating stuff, but I had never really stopped long enough in one place to smell the corporate coffee. I was proud of my achievements, defined by me as never having left a place without having recorded success as measured in the conventional corporate ways – but also never having left a place without feeling a genuine sense that the bulk of the people I was leaving were sorry to see me go. But I was beginning to feel uncomfortable, a discomfort that would see me leave Big Corporate life, by my own choice, within four years of seeing that billboard.

Part of that feeling was that my rapid progress had masked some very unconventional approaches to the task of managing a big chunk of corporate business. It wasn't just a case of getting away with it – in many ways some of it was a *cause* of my success. Although I dressed in a suit, I didn't always think or behave in a uniform way, and it paid dividends. Sometimes. There were downsides, as some of my behaviour was outrageous – but I usually moved on or up before those particular chickens came home to roost.[8]

---

[8] In 1984, in the UK, I was headhunted out of Whitbread by GrandMet. Immediately after I left, Whitbread produced a small brown booklet, which was given to all management and staff. It had a title like *Whitbread: Managing With Class And Integrity* (or some such bollocks). To this day the timing intrigues me.

More than once a peer had called me a Nutter. On a few occasions, a brave subordinate, encouraged by my 'first-name' management style, had called me a Nutter. On an even less number of occasions, a wiser boss had hinted the same thing.

Like most guys in their forties, I started asking questions of my shaving mirror. Most of the consequences of this process do not belong here, but should rather be buried deeply in a women's magazine as a prime case study. One aspect that intrigued me was my propensity for Nutterness. Was this the real me? Badly forcing the square peg of a barking non-corporate animal into the hole of a senior businessman?[9] Or was it something more subtle – a conventional businessman cleverly harnessing a talent for Nutterness as part of a broad range of technical and personal skills to achieve success? For a while, I thought it was the latter.[10]

So, this was where the self-interest came in. I started to track Nutters and Nutterness, in the hope that I could learn something.

I was looking for examples where controlled Nutterness would make someone (i.e. me if I transferred the example to my world) a better leader. My ingoing position was that all Nutterness would do so, but I quickly found out that the science (or art, you choose again) was dangerous. It could go off in your own hands, with hugely damaging consequences. But I also found it could work positively and spectacularly. In fact, few of the truly great business leadership stories of our time have been achieved *without* a least a teaspoonful of Nutterness. There was method in the some of the madness.

What I also found was that I couldn't get a handle on it unless I figured out what a modern business leader's *actual role was*. This was an amusing episode, as I had been one for many years – presumably without knowing. I had also attended one of the UK's finest business

---

[9] I have just re-read this sentence. It sounds obscene. I hope you know what I meant.
[10] Man, was I wrong.

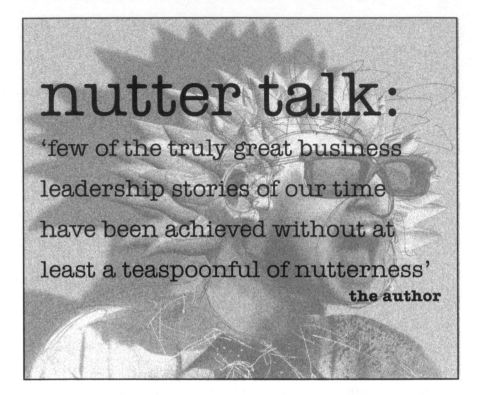

nutter talk:
'few of the truly great business leadership stories of our time have been achieved without at least a teaspoonful of nutterness'
the author

schools, emerging without a clue on this subject. So I worked it out for myself.

III WHAT SHOULD LEADERS DO?

As I write this, General Electric is facing the thought of life without Jack Welch. This will be like the E Street Band without Bruce Springsteen. In the eyes and minds of many commentators, Jack has been the business leader of business leaders in the Age of Aquarius. The company's earnings per share have gone through the roof during his time at the helm, and – judged by any conventional business success criteria – he has been The Man.

As he hands the weighty baton on to his chosen successor ('Top *that*, buddy') we may pause and reflect that we may never see a business leader of his stature again.

Jack Welch is not a Nutter. He is a Bright Focused Smiling Nasty Bastard – which is another animal entirely. The reasoning that draws me to the conclusion that he may be the last of his kind is that he had an involved executive role in all substantive aspects of GE, and it is my belief that the major companies of tomorrow are going to be just too big and complex to have one person conducting the orchestra. Michael Dell, who *is* a Nutter, has already recognised this, and runs Dell with a three-person-strong Office of the Chairman.

Consider the elements that may make up a modern international organisation. For the sake of brevity I'll limit myself to ten. Here goes:

- Source of corporate financing. Equity or debt, or some hybrid varietal? Which stock exchange(s) do you list on? What's your optimal share float? Should you issue more or buy some back? What's the message to investors and sector commentators?
- Range of products and services. If you are lucky enough to be appointed to lead the Sara Lee Corporation, you will need to make decisions affecting the frozen food products that bear the parent brand name – plus Hanes underwear, Wonderbras, Kiwi shoe polish, Champion sportswear, Ball Park frankfurters and Coach leather goods. In GE, the range is enormous – from scientific

products to financial services. In Gillette, from razors to batteries. Very few of the Big Guys stick to the knitting now, and every product has its own skill needs.

- Oh, and by the way, each product needs continual research and development. If its a high-tech product, that might now run into $ billions. You wouldn't want to get *that* decision wrong, would you?

- Sourcing raw materials and services. In-house or outsourced? Home or abroad? Should you control it or let somebody else? Every move you make trips a currency issue or a labour issue or a political issue. Or all of the above and more. How do you avoid the Nike Fuck-Up?

- Increasing regulation. Everywhere you exist, in any form, there is national, state or local government, or a statutory authority, or a consumer body, or *all* of the above – whose sole job seems to be to block your next move.

- How do you balance shareholders interests with your other stakeholders? How do you balance short term against long term? If times are hard, do you eat your seed-corn?

- How many markets can you support properly? Where do you attack? Where *must* you defend?

- How and where do you report profit? Sod GAAP, how *much* profit (or loss) do you report? What are the international taxation implications?

- How do you sell and how do you market your products and/or services? There are 50 ways to leave your lover (Paul Simon). There are now about fifty million ways to reach your target market (Barry Gibbons). How do you balance real and virtual trading?

- How do you develop an effective and efficient Information Technology and Telecommunications game plan for your company? This stuff *eats* money. How much do you spend? How do you measure its success?

- How do you attract, retain and develop winning people? Those nine words represent the biggest single challenge facing many corporations.
- Should you buy, or be bought by, or merge with, or jointly venture with, another company? Should such a move be to consolidate or diversify? Would it be to defend or aggress? Would it be upstream or downstream?

I said ten, and twelve it is. See? You can trust nobody.

You, in turn, can add as many more as you want. The point is that these organisations are getting too complex for one person to lead if leadership mandates the ability to add value to each of the above. The control-freak leader, sticking his or her oar into every decision, is heading for history's dumpster.

Does this mean fewer Nutters? *Au contraire*, I think we might see more of them. I do think the increasing size and complexity of companies has big implications for the corporate leadership role, and the climate might be right for an explosion of future Nutterness. It may become even less of an art and even more of a science. We may see it on the syllabus at business schools. Within five years, we will see Nutterness For Dummies on the shelves of bookstores.[11]

The corporate leadership role, I believe, will polarise into two elements. There is no question that the leader will still paint a picture of what the future might look like for the company. Some would call this shaping the vision. Others, inspired by *Star Trek*, would call it the mission. After that, however, my belief is that the leader will become less involved in *what* the company does to get there, and more involved in *how* it goes about the journey.

I need to sit down a minute. I need to hold on to something. I feel a sound bite coming on.

---

[11] Unless I write it before then.

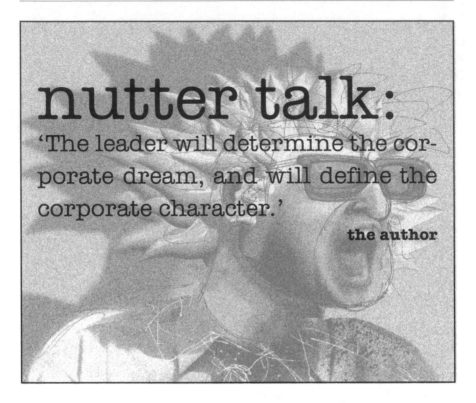

nutter talk:
'The leader will determine the corporate dream, and will define the corporate character.'
the author

The leader will determine the corporate dream, and will define the corporate character.

He or she then puts good people in place to deliver what's needed, and gets out of their way. It's happening now, and it will happen more in the future.

Now, here's the odd thing. It has also been the way of the business world in the past, the only difference being one of degree as past leaders have been much more involved in the day-to-day 'running' of companies. It has also had much to do with the development and triumph of Nutterness. What bit me high on the inner thigh was the realisation that it is in the execution of one or both of those two fundaments of leadership that past Nutterness flourished.

Let's look at the both of them.[12] A better understanding will give us a frame of reference against which we can look at examples. We may then be able to figure out if and where there was method in the madness.

---

[12] This may sound incorrect, but I can assure you that looking at the both of anything is perfectly normal in most parts of Ireland, and I'm thinking of book sales in the lucrative Emerald Market. Besides, my dad was after being from Limerick. Is that a great way of speaking, or what?

IV DREAM MERCHANTS

I don't like the idea of a leader coming up with visions or missions for the business. I will admit that part of that is purely personal. When I took over Burger King Corporation in 1989, it was after one of the last contested corporate acquisitions of the eighties. In these gladiatorial events, the eventual winners were, understandably, less than popular with the losing company's executives – although usually *very* popular with the losing company's shareholders. During such a process, the defending management team, and its advisers, would usually fight back with anything and everything they could lay their hands on.[13] A by-product of this would be the assembly of a lot of stuff that would be hugely embarrassing if it was left hanging around when the eventual winners – who would also be the new bosses – arrived on site.

When the dust had settled on our corporate 'victory', and I strode proudly through the door into my newly acquired office in Miami (and then I strode another 100 yards or so to my desk, upon which I could have landed a troop-carrying helicopter), I found, as expected, all the drawers and cupboards empty. The losing management team, having exhausted all attempts to fight off the predatory bid, had scorched the corporate earth[14] of documents on the way out. The only piece of paper left was a framed Pillsbury Mission Statement,[15] hung on the office wall. It looked forlorn and lonely. It was so full of crap and humbug that, there and then, I invented a new word to describe the language used in mission and 'values' statements. *Crumbug.*

---

[13] Frequently this would include a thinly disguised character assassination of the predatory company's senior executives. The incoming Burger King CEO (i.e. me) was described as a 'pub manager!' I enjoyed that.

[14] Or, in this case, the luxury carpet, imported from Italy. Or that may have been the sofa.

[15] Pillsbury was the parent company of Burger King Corporation in 1989, when the UK's GrandMet acquired the whole group.

Apart from there being more split infinitives in it than you could shake a stick at, the irony was gorgeous – and triggered my first mutinous thought against this practice. If they – the leaders of Pillsbury/Burger King – had governed according to their articulated creed, I wouldn't have been there reading it.

My second mutinous thought followed a nanosecond later. It centred on the Crumbug. Before that, and since then, I have known many leaders of all shapes and sizes in business. The amount of time they have spent on Crumbug is incredible. Fanned by a logic which, in itself, is sound enough – that everybody in and associated with the company must have a common understanding of where the company is going and what it stands for – they spend days (and sometimes hundreds of thousands of consultancy dollars) wordsmithing these goopy documents.

That is not the best use of a leader's time. It is not what the great leaders do best. It was what professors of English do best.

The great leaders have a *dream*. The best of their dreams don't need fancy words; they can be drawn *in crayon*. The Gold Medal leadership dream is one that can be crayoned, is one that nobody else has had, and – when the leader has crayoned it and shown it to somebody else – is one that elicits the response: *'With all due respect, boss, and I say this with all the reverence in the world: that idea is fucking NUTS'.*

I had a dream in Burger King. Fairly early on I recognised that sandwich for sandwich, location for location, price for price, marketing campaign for marketing campaign, it was difficult to get a *sustainable* competitive advantage. But we had over 250,000 people working somewhere in Burger King every day. The industry was (and still is) notorious for poor, front-line service – with low pay, low motivation, low self-respect and (consequently) high staff turnover.

Here was my dream. I saw a Burger King company in which *everybody gave a shit*. If I could have delivered it, Burger King would be without peer. The lawyers, of course, asked me to tone it down

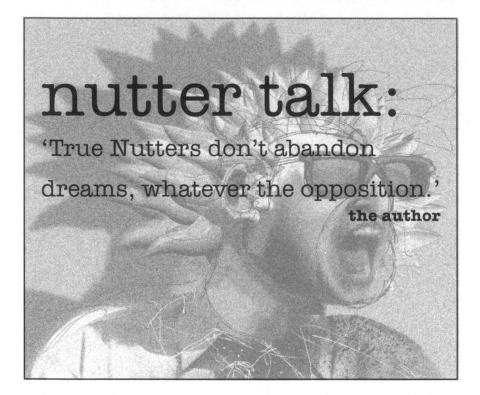

nutter talk:

'True Nutters don't abandon dreams, whatever the opposition.'

the author

a tad. Particularly if it was to go on network TV. The collective wisdom was that it was (or I was) Nuts. It could never be. The Burger King turnaround would be based on new products, better marketing, more locations, better buying, international expansion and blah-de-blah-de-blah. So, I abandoned my dream, and did all that stuff and got myself on the front cover of Fortune magazine. It is also why I'm writing this book and not in it. True Nutters don't abandon dreams, whatever the opposition. It may also be why you are reading it.

I'm convinced this dream thing is the primary job of a leader. Bill Gates, for all his prowess as a code-writer, was driven by a dream. He saw a PC on every table in every home and in every business in the world. He saw this when nobody else did – and it was this dream that drove him to develop[16] an operating system that could be used by such a market. A Quick and Dirty Operating System, or DOS as it became known.

I have heard this talent described – and I can't remember where, so somebody out there is now probably girding up to sue me – as *'Seeing shapes, at the horizon, between the earth and the sky, where the rest of us don't see anything'*. That works for me. More to the point for this thesis, it is most *the* most fertile ground for Nutters.

True Nutter-Shapes, for business, don't have to be about seeing something that was not there before. They don't have to be about new inventions. They can be about profound change to, or the re-invention of, something existing. Instead of a sweet cake, you can re-mix the same ingredients and make a savoury pie. What they do have in common is that they blow up the *status quo*. I'll make the illustrative point here with an example from another world – that of music. In the mid-1960s, Bob Dylan had assumed, in every way, the role and mantle of Woody Guthrie. The *genre* he chose was that of his dying mentor – poetic articulation, the recital of life-on-the-road experience and anti-Establishment blue-collar populism. For such a *young* artist to have succeeded, to such a degree and almost without qualification, was astonishing. The folk world lay at his feet. Then, for some reason known only to himself, at the Newport Folk Festival in 1965, he threw it all way. He appeared with an electric guitar and backed by a rock band. The purists hooted their derision.

History shows, of course, he didn't throw it all way. What he did was to create a whole *new genre* called folk rock. In business terms, yup, he lost some customers. But he not only reinvented himself and widened his *aggregate* market appeal, but he actually grew

---

[16] When I say 'develop' I mean he nicked it. I have included Gates here to illustrate the point, but I have not included him in the examples we will look at in more detail. For those, I have tried to select a bunch where, if we are talking about Dream-Nutters, their dreams were so unique that nobody else came near – either ever since or for a long time afterwards. In Gates's case, I suspect a herd of nerds was just behind him. Besides, he's boring and I've got to write this thing.

the total market. He achieved that by seeing a shape that everybody thought was Nuts. He was a Nutter all right, but there was a method in the madness. It gave him a forty-year career and icon status in one of the most competitive businesses on the planet.

We are going to look at some business people who were Nutters like Dylan. When their eyes close, they see these weird future shapes that you and I don't, or can't, see. We'll call them Dream Merchants.

First, we'll explore the idea that there is another category of Nutter.

nutter talk:

'branding is fertile ground for Nutters and Nutterness'

the author

V HOWBOYS

If *Dream Merchants* throws up some good Nutters, so does my second category – *HowBoys*.

In modern corporate life, it is becoming increasingly difficult to distinguish between the company and the brand. In times past, a brand was a product – soap powder, for example – and it was sold on specification or price. It was made in factories or assembly plants that represented major investments by the company's stockholders. Today, the science of branding is much more complex, and in many corporations the 'value' of the brand far exceeds the value of any tangible assets[17] found conventionally on the company balance sheet. The company may not even have any factories anymore – as in the case of Nike where, amidst much publicity – most of it adverse – they have outsourced production to anonymous third-world specialist[18] production companies.

To complicate matters further, a brand doesn't have to be a product anymore. Some are, for sure – Coca-Cola remains one of the world's great brands and it is a product (of sorts). Increasingly, however, services are becoming branded – led by such as American Express, America Online and Vodaphone. Again, this causes the accountants to have heartburn because these are things you can't stock-count (and, therefore, value) at the end of an accounting period.

How does this fit in with Nutterness? The art of branding is now becoming the essence of the science of managing *the whole business*. It also happens that branding is fertile ground for Nutters and Nutterness.

---

[17] Defined by the author as something you can kick. This definition has not yet been taken up by the GAAP authorities but it may well be.

[18] In many of these cases, 'specialist' means: '*Able to recreate worse working conditions – by a distance – than those existing in Lancashire, England, during the early part of the Industrial Revolution*'.

Take the premise one step further. The art of branding is about achieving *distinction*. It is not about better or worse specification, higher or lower price or inferior or superior quality – it is about being memorably different. If we follow this logic on a bit further, we find the base of one of the fundamental changes in management psyche over the last few years. Because *real distinction is hard to find.*

Almost every modern market is competitive and cluttered, and if it isn't it should be. I pointed out earlier a range of possible daily exposures to brand 'messages' for the 'average' western consumer. It might be as low as 3000, or as high as 30,000. I can understand either – I guess the first if you are largely housebound, the second if you travel a lot, read print media avidly, watch some TV and surf the Net. The last one is me. I said I can *understand* them, but I find them both frightening. The message is clear. Naomi Klein summarises it wonderfully: our lives are *stuffed with stuff.*[19]

So, it's hard to get sustainable distinction. Trying it on price won't last for long, and few can price-cut their way to long-term corporate prosperity. Distinct product specifications – even with patent protection – don't last long today. The key to distinction is moving away from *what* you do to *how* you do it. The pub manager who buys and sells beer finds it difficult to gain market distinction on beer product names and price. So he employs topless barmaids. You can see it's not that new an idea.

Sir Richard Branson,[20] leader of Britain's only (albeit self-proclaimed) new global brand in the last fifty years, throws some light on what's happening. To him, Virgin's distinction in the market place has little to do with the price of an airline seat, or the specification of a cola drink. At every available opportunity, Virgin – with a seamless join between the brand and the company – try to support a

---

[19] *No Logo,* Naomi Klein, Flamingo, HarperCollins 2000.
[20] This man does fascinate me. I have high respect for what he has achieved, and for his undoubted intuition. But sometimes when I see that bearded face in (yet another) facile photo opportunity, I reflect that, sometimes, there just isn't enough vomit in the world.

series of intangible attributes that they want to be seen to stand for – *great value, fun and innovation*. Their message is that if they can position the brand/company under an umbrella like that, then people who are comfortable with these values will try the products. Then you hook 'em.

The Distinction War is moving away from substance to style. Hard qualities like price and specification are being qualified and clouded, deliberately, by soft attributes like corporate character and personality. It is stuff that aims to makes you feel good, as a customer, when you think about the brand. This may boil down to a few *people* you know in the company – who may be the folk you transact with, as a customer, on a day-to-day basis. Or it may, of course, be the high-profile leader you see frequently in the media. It *feels* like you know him or her just as well.

This thesis does not assume you can win and keep business with bad prices and/or bad products. It does assume that companies that survive in this goofy world have competitive products and prices. What it adds to the gaiety of the whole thing is the idea that, to win over anything but the short term, you need to add another dimension. Somehow, you need to illustrate or articulate what you stand for as a business entity. You need to tell the consuming world this is *how* we do what we do. To this end, it helps enormously if your leader is a high profile HowBoy.

This is, of course, a Nutter's Charter. Although I believe it is increasing in importance and will continue to do so, it is not entirely new. Past Nutters have realised it, and plied their odd trade accordingly.

Dream Merchants and HowBoys. These people are far from being just oddballs or eccentrics. If we can find some Nutters that relate to those ideals we may find that they knew – all along – exactly what they were doing.

That is fine and, I hope, entertaining in and of itself. What I also want to examine, however, as we look more deeply into the ends that followed the Nutty means, and the method in the madness, is the idea that some of it could help us. Are any of these skills and/or idiosyncrasies transferable? Could a version of them – watered down if necessary and disguised if need be – help us all in our mundane business challenges?

Business, today, is full of grey processes churning about in a grey building. Grey leaders manage grey subordinates. Fewer people do more work with less leisure. A few winners create undreamed of wealth for themselves, while everybody else lives on debt. The price of making a mistake is the same as for failing – so the two have become blurred. Everybody is paranoid. Humour is as popular as smoking, and risk-taking is now surgically removed, at the company's expense in fairness, from anybody reaching middle management.

In the almost-forgotten words of the pop song – *Is this all there is?* I mean, *does it have to be like this?* God, I hope not. As my contribution to the de-greying of the business world, I am hoping there are some things we can learn (and steal) from these folks. If nothing else, before we go under, we can all throw our toys out of the pram.

LUCIANO BENETTON

WE MAY AS WELL START with the guy who triggered the whole thing off with me. We'll examine him as a Dream Merchant and a HowBoy, and see where he lands in the long jump sandpit. We'll use him as a first mark, and see how the rest compare.

The first thing we need to digest is that he has done far, far more in the cause of definitive Nutterness than hang a semi-nude billboard up next to Miami's most conservative fish restaurant.[1] Not only a lot more, but for a lot longer. By my calculation, if we are talking about these guys seeing 'shapes' the rest of us don't see, he

---

[1] Er ... it's the restaurant people who are conservative, not the fish

can make a case for having seen five of them, stretching over five decades.

You will see when you come to the next chapter (on James Dyson) that I don't know what solipsism means. I assume you are the same, so I won't bore you with much stuff about me. I do, however, want to go back in time to set a scene. This scene is going back long enough in time to be a black and white memory for me, but that does nothing to reduce its clarity and impact.

Post-war Europe was a battered, broken, dark cold place. At least that's my memory. As we entered the 1950s my dad had just endured a decade which would try the patience of a saint. Married just before the start of World War II, he was whisked off within days of his wedding to the Far East with the British army. My mother didn't see him again until 1945, when he arrived back in England after surviving Japan's gracious hospitality as a prisoner of war. He weighed, I think, less than ninety pounds. I was born in the first full year of peace, but fate then dealt him another crushing blow as my mother died when I was just three.

He had a job to keep up, so we sort of twinned up like the Ancient Mariner and the Albatross, and went about our collective lives. One thing he did to over-compensate was spoil me something rotten. Which is how I come to remember Barrys (or Barries – my memory is not *that* good), Manchester's high-end clothing retailer of the day. He bought *all* my clothes there.

It is difficult today to imagine post-war European clothes stores. Even if you were there, and experienced it, it now seems as though it was on another planet, in an entirely different space-time continuum. Now that we are used to bright department stores or GAP-like emporia, it seems positively Dickensian to those who do remember it – or to those who listen in acute boredom when somebody like me describes it with their eyes half closed.

There was always a big, dark, wood counter, clearly defining what was your approved space as a customer, and that of the shop assistants. Little or no clothing was on display. Shirts, woollen goods and socks (etc.) were kept in drawers behind the counter. When you asked for such an item, the response would be: '... and which shade of grey would you like, sir? Mid-grey, dark-grey or (disapproving glance) light-grey?' Somewhere in the back would be a range of tweed sports jackets and long winter overcoats (maybe with a radical navy blue thrown in amongst the greys). You ordered suits from one of four rolls of cloth (grey or blue with pinstripe, grey or blue without pinstripe).

I never went there, but I have it on good authority that, at the same sort of time, post-war Italy was even bleaker. Clothes retailing was even more restricted – with a person's job and social status governing what was worn. To add to the gaiety of that nation at that time, the economy was shattered, with the vast majority of the population living hand-to-mouth and from day-to-day.

It was the world of a teenage Luciano Benetton. Forced into an early adulthood with the death of his father at the end of the war, Luciano strived to be the breadwinner for his sister Giuliani, and his two younger brothers Carlo and Gilberto. He became an apprentice in a grim store selling clothes, and was astute enough to notice that his sister, charged with making most of their own clothes, made rather cool-looking woollen sweaters.

As the first of his Dreams starts to take a loose shape, it is fair to add that there was some kind of a following wind. Italian knitwear had a strong fashion heritage, and by 1952 some of the top Italian designers – Aponte, Arditi, Galliani and Mariangelo – were giving Paris a run for its money. So there was a kind of latent cultural flair, hanging about post-war Italy, waiting for somebody to release it. (This sort of thing was not wildly evident in post-war Manchester.) Then the Marshal Plan and the UN reconstruction and rehabilitation administration began to prop up the Italian economy.

It was 1956 before the first Dream picture began to crystallise. The twenty-year-old apprentice clothes retailer began to feel frustrated on every front. In his imagination, clothes retailing was different. There was no big territory-defining counter. Young people

would shop without their parents. Clothes would be casual and colourful. They would be visible within the shop, and accessible in
price. This sounds bora-bora-bora today, but in the 1950s it was an
animal that simply did not exist.

I typed that last paragraph at my fastest speed.[2] I did that in
the silly hope that some of that velocity would inflect itself into the
way you read it, and you would pass it by quickly. By doing this you
would not really digest its content and implications. So, now we will
go back and take it a bit more slowly. That paragraph (beginning 'It
was 1956' and ending 'did not exist') is pivotal – not just to Luciano,
but to Nutterness in general.

What we had is an ordinary guy, working in a place and in a
business not of his choosing. His family business was renting bicy-
cles, but the death of his father, the ravages of war and the need for
a steady income for his family had seen him grab a job in the clothes
store. Then, to this young man comes a vision, which turns everything about the traditional and conventional ways of going about
a clothes-retailing business inside out. Why him? Why then? Why
there? Where did the inspiration come from? If you are like me, and
if you were in those circumstances at that time, you would not have
had that vision if it had been the only way for you to escape from a
pack of wild dogs snapping at your genitals.

What we have is a *coming together*. I am going to liken it to a
jigsaw, an analogy you will see develop as we look at more of these
folk. By luck or judgement, circumstances or inspiration (or all of the
above), a number of pieces come together. Only one specific person
at one peculiar time has them all, and only he or she can fit the shapes
into one picture. It is, therefore, unique.

Benetton worked in an environment where so many things
were outdated; somebody was going to start making changes soon.
That applied to many industries in the post-war period. The fact he
was a bright guy and bored shitless helped him to take more ideas

---

[2] You don't want to know.

of change a lot further. At first, in his imagination, then for real. The economy was getting ready to provide the consumer world with the monetary weapons to break out of war-driven, rationing-driven austerity. There was a growing mood to end drabness in all its forms. And, at his home, Luciano had a trump card – a sister who was already making bright woollen clothes.

Although the shop-shape dream was in his mind from this time on, the product revolution came before the retailing revolution.

Around this time, Giuliani working at her old knitting machine, made a yellow jumper for one of Luciano's friends. The traditional colours for woollens at this time were grey,[3] blue and burgundy. It was the catalyst that the dreamer needed to start making it all real. With enormous personal sacrifice the family scraped enough money to buy a commercial knitting machine – the plan being that Giuliani would make 'em and Luciano would sell 'em. And sell them he did, culminating in an order from the shop in which he worked for several hundred jumpers. This marked the stage that moved them from amateurs to a family manufacturing business. All four siblings were soon joined together in the enterprise, and within eight years of the first yellow jumper, they were selling 20,000 of them a year.

By the mid-sixties, the next piece of the jigsaw was ready to go in place. One of Benetton's customers proposed a store *dedicated* to their products. Luciano was already showing early signs of another Nutter-calibre breakthrough shape – that of being an 'indirect' retailer, controlling the way his clothes were sold to the public while remaining as an upstream supplier. He latched onto the idea, and the first dedicated shop concept was born.

There was still a counter (the lease specified it had to stay – the world was not yet ready for its widespread death!) but it was painted in light colours. There were lots of pine shelves, and the enthusiastic supplier piled them high with red, blue, yellow, orange and green jumpers. The pitch was openly aimed generally at young shoppers,

---

[3] See? Manchester was right in line. . .

and specifically at females. It had the radical addition of a pretty girl assistant. It was a poor retail location, in Belluno in the hills of northern Italy. It was, nonetheless, a huge success. A second one followed rapidly, this time without the counter. Again, Luciano devolved responsibility for running the store, but kept creative control of it. Again it was a huge success. Soon after, these exclusive stores became branded as Benetton, and by the year 2000 there were 9000 of them.

There are two clear, independent Nutter-dreams here, and that's before we get to the interracial breastfeeding picture. To invent a completely new range of products and a completely new way of fashion retailing would be enough, for most people, for a couple of lifetimes. To invent a new corporate architecture in parallel, verges on being cheeky.

The development of franchising was not Benetton's breakthrough. By the 1960s many retail chains saw this as a way of rapidly growing brand distribution – notably the American fast-food giants. But there were to be, and to remain, important differences in these business models. With Benetton, there was no written contract. All clothes were supplied exclusively by Benetton on a no-return basis. The licensee paid no royalties – either as a brand fee or 'contribution' to marketing. A combination of the latter could add up to anything from 6–10% of sales annually – as it was in my old company, Burger King, and much more than that in some 'modern' franchised systems. Finally, a heavily weighted importance was put on the 'kind' of businessperson who wanted a license, as against those who could just come up with the money.

It was – is – a unique approach. It would cause problems in litigious America towards the end of the millennium, but there and then it provided Luciano with two things. First, a unique level of downstream control for somebody who was essentially just a supplier. Second, it meant he did not tie up cash by taking title to the goods in the retail store. Nor did Benetton tie up capital in owning the store itself. It meant, therefore, that capital would be left free to invest in more and more advanced systems of production, system control, communications and advertising.

The first three of these produced another unique Nutter shape. Benetton linked leading-edge information technology with a break-through automated distribution facility in Italy. It enabled the company to respond to the fact it wasn't a fast-food joint, and that fashion comes and goes rapidly. The company could respond to subtle or profound changes in demand faster than any competition – and virtually on a store-by-store basis.

The corporate structure also had another implication – that Benetton, the company, bore the cost of brand advertising. It therefore had *de facto* creative control, but the fact that it had no contributing licensee marketing fund meant that it had – comparatively – scarce funds, particularly to penetrate the US market. It needed some low-cost/high-impact marketing. Which is where we came in.

It was not until 1982 that Luciano Benetton met Oliviero Toscani, and a further eighteen months until the company began using his work. The son of a famous Italian photographer, he was already celebrated in the same field, with studios in New York and Paris. Home was a farmhouse in Tuscany. His work had already graced *Elle, Vogue* and *Harpers*, and he already had a reputation for being controversial. It is clear that there was an early meeting of minds, and that a friendship developed before they worked together – work that would result in Benetton becoming one of the five most recognised brands in the world. It is also clear that Toscani became Luciano's alter ego. What is less obvious, and sometimes lost in the emotion of this whole story, is that what triggered the advent of this Nutterness was boring old economics. Toscani's soul was the vehicle, but Luciano's hands were always on the steering wheel. It was a calm, calculated road headed for optimised effectiveness and efficiency of limited advertising funds that they took. Benetton simply did not have the conventional advertising dollars to penetrate the US market, its big target of the 1980s.

Toscani's first work gave only subtle hints of what was to come. In 1984 the 'All the Colours of the World' print and billboard campaign featured a group of smiling, ethnically diverse children, united by the colours of Benetton. He used real children, not models – again a foretaste of what was to come. The impact was immediate. With the exception of South Africa and some Neanderthal comments from a correspondent in Manchester, acclaim for the message of harmony was universal.

At this stage I would love to do no more than list the resultant sequence of Toscani's work for Benetton, throwing a few picture examples in as illustration. That would be much more than a page filler. Unless you had a heart of stone, it would warm your day and lighten your personal burdens, particularly if I limited the exercise to his 'golden period' of the late 1980s. But this is about Luciano Benetton, not Olivieri Toscani, and we need to note and register two things here.

We need to remind ourselves, first, that this was a cold, clinical commercial decision. Benetton knew that Toscani never was, and never would be, about advertising *clothes*. The closest Toscani got to that was to use Benetton as a vehicle to push the world to a new way of living and thinking. Benetton was astute enough to see the impact that this could have for his brand. Secondly, he was brave enough – Nuts enough – to realise there could be no halfway house. He had to let Toscani's genius take the brand with him on his journey. Years later, reflecting on this aspect in a BBC TV interview[4] Luciano remembered his briefing speech to Toscani: 'Don't let anybody stop you, *not even me*'.

The campaigns became increasingly controversial, and the US licensees (in particular), who began suffering from increased competition and some brand fatigue in the 1990s, began to see Toscani as one of Benetton's problems not solutions. In the early 1990s, the image of a (just) dead AIDS victim resulted in the beginning of a se-

---

[4] *Blood On The Carpet*, aired on 8th January 2001.

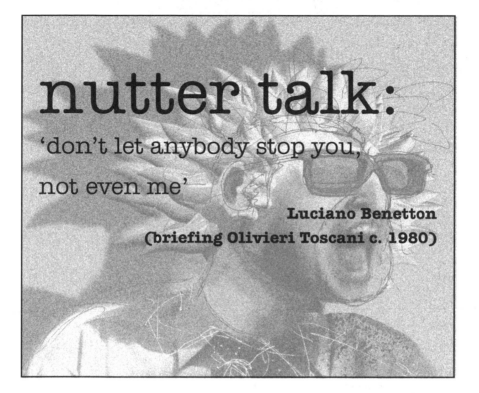

nutter talk:

'don't let anybody stop you,

not even me'

Luciano Benetton
(briefing Olivieri Toscani c. 1980)

ries of international store-based protests. By the end of the decade, with the US reduced to less than 200 stores from a previous peak of 600, Toscani's images to support the heralded brand rebirth brought matters to a head.

Backed by his European distaste for the American practice of murdering its convicted murderers, he produced a $10.0 million campaign based on the faces of convicted criminals on Death Row. Seeing the face of the guy who had murdered their child plastered on billboards – ostensibly selling jumpers – upset an American man and wife so much they began a protest. As it can in America, it snowballed and Sears cancelled a contract that would have put Benetton inside 400 of their department stores. Luciano pulled the campaign, and fired his old friend and alter ego. In doing so he got rid of the man who – maybe more than anybody – had catalysed the explosion in the growth of Benetton's brand awareness and positioning. I repeat: he fired him. What a Nutter.

There's one I have left out here – but you must be as bored as I am with this guy's ability to just go flat out in the face of received wisdom and convention time after time. It could be argued that he was instrumental in the 'store within a store' concept of retailing, whereby a brand will take a concession within a bigger department store. If he didn't invent it, he was a major player in developing it into the widespread practice we are all aware of today. But even if I skip that, we've done enough to establish a pattern. Time and time again, he saw and produced a shape, a game plan that nobody else saw. Time and time again, he looked in his personal jigsaw box, saw what pieces he had and pieced them together in a way that was unique to him and the world outside. Nobody else had pieces that were quite that shape, nobody else could make that picture.

He is a Dream Merchant of the highest calibre, of that I have no doubt.

It is also my observation that he is a HowBoy to be reckoned with, and this may be less obvious. Here we need to sow the seeds of a rather contentious theory – that Nutterness supporting what a company stands for – *how* it goes about doing what it does – is not just about touchy-feely people skills, empowerment, good communications and dress-down Fridays. It may not always be nice. What we are concerned about is whether it worked or not.

Luciano Benetton is a shadowy character. He spurns the personal limelight as do his siblings and, by now, numerous children, nephews and nieces. The structure of the (still) family-run group of companies would appear to be designed to confuse, to hide, to duck and to dive. There is an air of mystery about all the principal players and their inter-relationship. But if you look at how Luciano conducts himself, you see the company's personality mirrored. It is about emotion and lifestyle not product; it is about control without ownership, it is about a preparedness to offend the few to attract the many – but leave nobody with *no opinion* about the brand. It is about the old being ruthlessly discarded for the new, even if that means saying goodbye to deep and synergistic friendship. Some Nutters are in this book for one crazy Dream, this guy had maybe five. Just as important, he was, is, and looks as though he will remain for some time, the *soul* of Benetton.

NUTTER SCORE:

Dream Merchant: Five stars (out of five)

HowBoy: Four stars (out of five)

JAMES DYSON

2

I STARTED DELIBERATELY WITH A SURE-FIRE NUTTER. Even if you don't agree with my conclusions, I think you would agree that Benetton is one of the world's high-profile businessmen. His dream(s) and his method(s) are fodder for endless debates over cocktails in every capital city, and provide case studies in business schools in every country. He has also been a Nutter for a long time.

Not much of the above applies to the second guy on my batting list. I know before I start that this Nutter will score differently. But I don't know whether his mark in the sandpit will be longer or shorter, or whether it will be left or right of Luciano's imprint. At this stage I don't even know if he's jumping in the same pit.

I now need to declare my prejudices. You will find me doing this a lot in this book. In the case of James Dyson, I am stating upfront that he gets on my tits.

This rather unacademic position is the result of three factors, none of which should objectively reflect on the merits of his case to be a high quality Nutter of some category or other. But I am the jury here, and you need to know that, had I presented myself for jury duty in the normal way, I would have been sent straight home.

First factor: I thought a good place to start would be Dyson's autobiography. On the bookshelf, it winked its title at me: *James Dyson, An Autobiography: Against The Odds.*[1] I read it, but (as you do) skipped the preface and introduction. I was humbled – not only is the guy a genius, and a fighter – but he is *so articulate.* Just look at the opening:

> *'Though writing an autobiography, I am not so terminally af-flicted by solipsism as to think you will want much of my parents, birth, and what J.D. Salinger called "all that David Copperfield kind of crap".'*

That is punchy stuff for a self-confessed vacuum cleaner developer/ salesman. Solipsism, by the way, is defined in my dictionary as 'the philosophical theory that the self is the only knowable, or the only existent, thing'. I had no idea – so I've saved you the trouble of looking it up.

Then, much as I do everything in life ass-backwards, I went back to the front of the book and read the preface. He didn't write it. Giles Coren, the increasingly famous writer-son of the famous writer-father wrote it, using as a source a series of 'long hours of [Dyson's] rambling'. Now, I don't have a problem with ghost writers. It's an honourable profession, and has brought many stories into the public domain that would otherwise have stayed dark. But I have a

---

[1] Texter Publishing Limited , 1997.

problem in using one and calling the result an *auto*biography. I don't care what the legal publishing position is, what we have is an approved biography. As much of the Dyson success story is based on Dyson's rhetoric and ability to talk about his technical products, every time I hear him, or read about him or about his products, the word 'autobiography' now flashes in front of my eyes. And it will forever.

Second prejudice: notwithstanding 'autobiography', the guy is a technical and scientific genius. Whatever the mathematical opposite is of that, I am it. In my last science exams, back in (I think) 1962, I scored less in percentage terms than teachers and nurses normally get for an annual pay rise. I have, therefore, a healthy disrespect for *anybody* who knows what a pipette is.

Again, for the benefit of those who know me not, I repeat my stance on a basic scientific tenet – that somewhere, *somewhere*, in a box of tissues, *there is a battery*. When you pull one out, another tissue pops up, and I know that such things don't happen in modern life without a teeny-weeny battery somewhere inside. Trust me. But show me a guy who can explain all this on a chalkboard, and I will show you somebody who could bore for his country. At the bar, I am attracted to those who eat potato chips, not those who talk of those made from silicone. As far as I am concerned, Dyson is one of *them.*

Third factor. We haven't had, and don't have, a Dyson product in either our US or English house. The acquisition of one is not, as far as I know, on our radar screen. That is less understandable in the UK, because the hype and the success are now ever-present, and we are of the kind who would support British industry given half a choice. But we haven't got one. There is a reason, and I don't know it. My wife is the Holder Of The Reason, just as she is the Holder Of Many Others. But I'm not going to ask her. Just take it from me; there is *some flaw* in the whole act somewhere. Somehow.

Enough prejudices.

This is different from Benetton. I'm going to start by making two daft generalisations here – which will tick off a few of you. First, that I will be addressing a largely male audience. That is a simple (and sad)[2] fact about the demographics of business-book-buying audiences. In which case, as a man, you will know *precisely* fuck-all about hoovers (notice the small 'h' in hoovers – it's important, trust me and read on). Second generalisation – some of you, if my publisher has done his job, will be reading this outside the UK. In which case you will know exactly the same about Dyson and Dysons.

The guy re-invented the Hoover. The machine was so synonymous with the mighty corporation that largely led its development, it became, aspirin-like, one of those products that get named after the company. The company was Hoover; the product was a hoover. Electrolux sells Electrolux hoovers.

In Dyson's story, the technical (re)invention is one thing. Making it a success in modern times, against all odds (and giant corporations, sceptical backers and endless lawsuits) is another. Both parts are astonishing. The Dream part of the journey of the Dyson Dual Cyclone (aka Not A Hoover) lasted from its technical genesis in 1978 until it hit the market in 1993. Compare that with my invention of a battery-operated snooker/pool cue about the same time, which (as yet) shows no signs of taking the snooker world – or any other come to that – by storm.

Fifteen years. What must have seemed like a million years to him is in fact a microsecond on the scale of historic commercial development – it took hundreds of years to find something that would measure longitude while at sea. And Burger King *still* can't get the French fries right.

Whether it was a long time or a flash, depending on your perspective, there was one consistent barrier to progress. Almost everybody exposed to the project voiced a common challenge: that if a better kind of vacuum cleaner were possible, *then Hoover or Electrolux would have invented it*. At this stage we record that he not only

---

[2] My goal is to change this. My next book will be called, *The First Five Million Male Snafus in Business History – Vol. 1*, (First of a LONG series).

invented it, developed it, launched it – he still owns it. It now outsells Hoover in the UK, despite costing substantively more. It is creeping across the word. He actually sells it to Japan. Yes, you read correctly – Japan imports some consumer electronics. It's his dream come true, and what a dream.

My prejudices notwithstanding, we will consider this guy as a high-quality Dream Merchant. My prejudices, however, will not allow me to consider him as a HowBoy of any kidney. He champions much of the dress-down, empowery, touchy-feely stuff in his business, but I can tell from here he's just splashing about in the shallow end. That's not why he's batting second in this book.

If we clear our minds and concentrate on him as a Dream Merchant, we begin to see some factors with him that we saw in Benetton. They are consistent enough to give a base for analysis in others, and (maybe) some subsequent theorising. So, I'm going to sew some seeds about Dream Merchants right here and right now. They will appear with a frequency that might surprise those who believe that these folk are unfathomable. I want to take a first tilt at the idea these folk are eccentrics, who produce a crazy rabbit out of a crazy hat at a time that proved fortuitous but unplanned by anyone other than some smirking deity. What is important about that is the implication for you. Breakthrough dreaming may, after all, be a science and not an art.

With Dyson, the Big Dream was not a blinding epiphany. He wasn't some paper-pusher walking down Damascus High Street, who was suddenly blinded by a (detailed) vision of a Dual Cyclone vacuum cleaner, complete with a final design specification and development-funding package. It is crystal clear to me, a low-tech Neanderthal, that the Dream 'shape' this guy came up with is genuine Nutter stuff – i.e. freakishly different and going against all conventional (aka industry) wisdom. It is equally clear that the vision did not appear from nowhere, and that it did not appear all at once.

Like Luciano Benetton, in my observation he put together *pieces of a jigsaw*. The end picture was unique, but the pieces that came together were not so, and there were not that many of them. What made the end picture a true breakthrough was that nobody had taken these particular pieces, or their own different ones, and put them together to form this picture, this shape. We've seen it twice now. It's a theme we will see repeated.

Dyson put together five pieces of his jigsaw, and produced the Dual Cyclone vacuum cleaner. They are worth looking at individually.

Jigsaw piece #1

Everybody has been influenced by somebody, to some degree. In all lives there are people who have been role models, mentors, teachers or idols. They may not have been close; there may not have been a physical relationship, or even contact of any kind. You may just have read their books, or read about them; seen them in movies or bought their records. You may have just heard about them, or seen them at work or play from a distance. They may not even be from the same era. You may not even be consciously aware of them and their contribution to the world – but, sure as hell, one way or another, to a greater or lesser extent, they have influenced you.

To many people, parents are the seminal influence, but few would admit to walking life's trail without further influences. In my case, Brendan Behan, Denis Law, Albert Finney, John Lennon and Tom Peters[3] all permeated my insular skin, and had varying effects on my attitude and behaviour. These influences are not, of course, necessarily of the 'action-reaction' kind. They can enter the human spirit and lie there, dormant, until circumstances merit their emergence.

With this in mind, let's look back at Dyson's evolution. *Voila*. In his college years, he is introduced to the works of Buckminster Fuller, eventual patentee (in 1954) of the geodesic dome – since reproduced

---

[3] Small wonder I did not reinvent the vacuum cleaner.

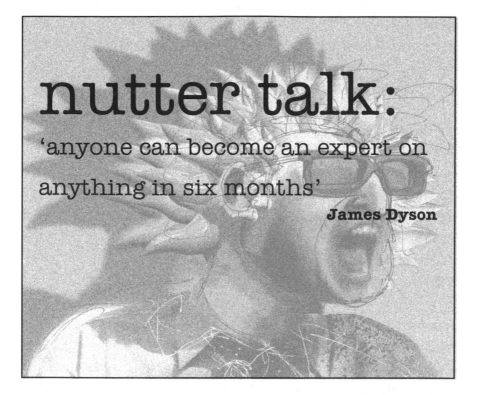

nutter talk:

'anyone can become an expert on anything in six months'

James Dyson

more than 300,000 times in sports arenas, subtropical housing and the permanent base at the South Pole. I'm not going into the technology here (save to say it works on the principle of an egg – a weak material put together in a super-efficient shape), but there are two important aspects of this guy's influence on Dyson that clearly get banked by him. He has already swallowed the fact that engineering is important in its own right. He has already swallowed the fact that design is important in its own right. But here he digests that the two together can be alchemic.

As if Fuller weren't enough, Dyson's primary admitted influence reinforces this whole idea – Isambard Kingdom Brunel. He (Dyson) spent much of his life in the shadow of Brunel's arched railway tunnel at Box (near Bath), and was deeply influenced by his genius in adapting existing engineering principles (i.e. bridges) to new uses (i.e. tunnels). But, maybe more than that, he digested Brunel's philosophy that just because something has never been done before, that needn't be a barrier. It could still be possible, it may even be probable. As icing on the cake, he also noted Brunel's insistence that he kept control of his projects.

I don't ask much of you in this book, but this point needs making heavily. Go back and read that last paragraph slowly. I've just done it – it takes a minute or so. Now, figure you are a young, bright guy, and you have these influences stored. They are just waiting for an appropriate set of circumstances to arrive, and they will emerge and set to work. There is one piece of the jigsaw in place, and we now need more.

Jigsaw piece #2

It is said that John Lennon couldn't leave a word alone. When the original (pre-Ringo) Fab Four were searching for a name, the me-too name of 'Beetles' was put forward. The me-too bit was aping the Crickets, Buddy Holly's group. Lennon got hold of it and changed it to Beatles, and the rest is history.

A mind that cannot leave things alone is a jewel of a thing, along with being an occasional pain in the backside if it belongs to your children. Have you ever thought about the *very* first time that man got milk out of a cow – what the hell was he doing? What's the mentality that drives somebody to go over to an animal twice or three times the size of a human[4] and pull on its udders, and then *drink* what comes out, when he (it was 'he', trust me) had no previous information on the subject?

There are guys who cannot leave things alone. Guys to whom the *status quo* is anathema. Dyson was and is one. Again, I'm not going to get too techie here, but we need to rewind his movie to late 1978, when he was working on the design and development of gar-

---

[4] Let's assume he at least got the sex right and pulled on a cow – the alternative doesn't bear thinking about.

den products. He was newly married and – to put it politely – broke. He shared domestic duties with his wife, including battling with a troublesome, inefficient, reconditioned Hoover Junior upright vacuum cleaner. During one particular bag changing ceremony, he noticed that the machine's efficiency improved with a new bag, but only for a short time.

So he did exactly what I, and the vast, vast, vast majority of you, would never have thought of doing. He cut it open to have a look-see. He deduced that there was a basic flaw in the bag technology in that the pores of the new bag became clogged up very quickly. After that – which happened when the bag was only partly full – efficiency tailed off. He then deduced that re-useable bags were permanently clogged, and disposable ones became so very early in their life. He then deduced there was a basic technical flaw in the bag system, and that there had been for a century. He then deduced that this annoyed him. I, and you, of course, would have deduced that the thing didn't work, put it back in the cupboard under the stairs and buggered off to watch Match of the Day.

The solution he came up with doesn't belong on this jigsaw piece. This just has painted on it that he has a mind that can't leave things alone.

Jigsaw piece #3

This is about transference skills. Not 'transferable skills', which are things sought after by HR departments – particularly when they are looking for shortlist candidates for general management jobs. The latter are skills that enable their owner to move, for example (and to quote a much travelled path) from accountancy into operations. Transference skills are different. Their owner may never move from being an engineer or a marketing guru (or whatever), but he or she can apply a solution that is working somewhere within that field to a problem that lies unresolved somewhere else within that field.

Now we go back to an angry Dyson stomping about the place complaining about his vacuum bag defect to anybody who would listen. The audience, I suspect, was limited. Some, I am sure, had they heard him might have suggested that he got a life.

As it happens, at this exact time, he was involved in producing wheelbarrows, which were sprayed with epoxy powder – which became a tough paint when baked. Huge amounts of this spray would miss, which would be collected up by the equivalent of a huge vacuum cleaner. This machine was even more inefficient doing its job than the domestic hoover-turkey he had at home. The spray-machine providers told him that big industrial users used a cyclone to handle the surplus material. Somebody pointed one out to him on a sawmill nearby. So – get this – while I was watching Match of the Day the following week, he climbed over the wall one night and copied it. He then rigged a thirty-foot cyclone up to do the job in his workshop. Sometime during this process, he remembered his Hoover Junior. He went home and made a cardboard cyclone, this time about twenty-nine feet smaller than his workshop model, and shoved it somehow (am I being too technical here?) either up or into his irritating vacuum cleaner. He then vacuumed the house – with full and maintaining efficiency – from top to bottom. He became (in his words) the only man in the world with a bagless vacuum cleaner. I am not aware of how he stilled his beating heart, but three pieces of the jigsaw were now to hand.

Jigsaw piece #4

Dyson did not go home that night and emerge ten hours later with one of those yellow and grey see-through jobbies, have a coffee, secure financing, build a production plant and launch it by lunch the following day. What happened next took fifteen years. We will see later that it doesn't have to take that long to launch a Nutter-Dream, but it does take a particular talent, and it's the one on this piece of the jigsaw. Every Dream will be different, but every one has its own critical path and the Nutter has to be prepared to see it right through, *whatever it takes*. There were to be five thousand prototypes of the Dual Cyclone vacuum cleaner before it was market-ready in 1993. The second cyclone didn't arrive until 1982.

Every genuine Nutter Dream has, by definition, built-in barriers to progress. Cynicism, comfort with what's existing, investment in what's existing, plain old jealousy, fear of the unknown, the 'it wasn't invented here' syndrome – and sometimes all, or combinations, of the above, make the journey a tough old odyssey. Dyson had them all in spades, and some I can identify with. Many times since I left big business, I have fronted potential investors. Their propensity to lie – openly and cheerfully – still astounds me. Most want to risk losing nothing on the downside, with the upside that they take over your business if you succeed. I faced one who kept repeating that the game was a game of 'golden rules' – i.e. that the guy with the 'gold' would be the guy that would make all the 'rules'. I looked it up in a language dictionary and then was delighted to tell him to fuck off in his native Cuban.

In the worst of these journeys it doesn't just take perseverance. It may be a complex technical breakthrough that's needed; it may be a fight with a partner that needs to be survived. A pilgrim's progress here can face a million obstacles, and need a whole array of skills as well as a teaspoon of bloody-mindedness. The point is that the Dreamer stays with it. Every day, he or she gets up and does what has to be done to get through to bedtime. He or she does whatever is needed to keep the Dream alive, and the process rolling forward. And then he or she repeats as necessary until the Dream lives. Whether that takes a week or fifteen years.

Jigsaw piece #5

The last piece is about comfort. On the surface, a strange element when compared to what's on the other four pieces, where comfort is distinctly lacking. It is, however, a weird comfort. It is a comfort

I haven't got, but have witnessed in many other people – particularly start-up entrepreneurs and potential Nutters. It is the comfort of having the whole ranch bet on one Dream.

Once you get a mortgage, you are supposed to move to the right in your personal politics. I have heard it said that if you ever get on a public bus after you are thirty years old, you have failed in life. These facile ideas are indirectly about a much more solid thesis – that success broadly equates with security. Whatever form it takes, I do know that a seminal force in many lives is to secure a home and a reasonable quality of life for one's family. Once achieved, that becomes untouchable. After that, well, a gamble is fun.

This is not the case with Nutter-Dreamers. Their gambles aren't fun. In many (most?) cases we will find there is no safety net. It may not be a whole house, it may be a whole reputation at stake – but whatever the stakes are, they are no half-measures. They are high and total. Winner takes all, loser loses all. This element is painted clearly on Dyson's fifth jigsaw piece. For fifteen years he lived hand-to-mouth, up to his armpits in debt, to bring this Dream home. It is a position I would hate to be in, but I believe Nutters can draw strength from it. For sure, as a buddy of mine used to say: 'the imminent presence of death focuses the mind' – and it can be a great motivator. I'm talking above and beyond that. I think some of these folks enjoy it.

We have assembled the five pieces of Dyson's jigsaw. We are considering him, remember, as a Dream Merchant. My observation is that he is one, and one of the highest quality. Few dreams must have seemed dafter at genesis than this, and few have had as many barriers thrown before them as they entered the real world from stage left. Few have been as successful, against all these odds.

So, what's special about the jigsaw? After all, you and I have pieces of our jigsaw that look, well, a bit like some of those belonging to Dyson – so how come my electric snooker cue didn't take off? It's quite simple. Only he had *all* these five pieces, and only he put them together *in a way that made his shape*. Nobody else saw it. I don't think anybody else could have seen it.

I said earlier we wouldn't even put him on the list for HowBoy analysis. I'm standing by that. Sure, he runs a no-suits, no-ties, no-memos business operation, yaps on about empowerment and serves salads in the factory cafeteria. But if how he runs his business is characterised by how he 'writes' his *auto*biography, I'm signing off here.

NUTTER SCORE:

Dream Merchant: Five stars

HowBoy: One star

MICHAEL DELL

W E ARE THREE INTO THIS SERIES, and I know I'm going to have a problem with this guy.

If you look at my list of Nutters, even assuming you accept the basic thesis, I'm sure you would want to make changes. Your own favourites would come in and a couple of my marginal ones would take a hike. I suspect, however, that with whatever list we would end up with, there would be a surprising range of characters. This would feed the theory that there isn't a single stereotype for a Nutter. They are not all extrovert and they are not all self-seeking egomaniacs.

Let's turn that thought around – and see if there are any personality traits that are consistent through their *absence*, and here it might seem easier to leap to a conclusion. Our Nutters may be different in many ways, but none of them are *boring*, correct?

Wrong. And here I give you Michael Dell. His Nutty idea turned conventional sales, marketing and distribution practices on their heads in his particular field. He probably accelerated the *total* market growth for his products and he left some big – and I mean BIG – competitors with their flies undone. He also changed forever the way all big companies must think about relating to their customers – whether they peddle goods or services, and whether they sell to other companies or to single, end-user consumers. Clearly he is bright as a button, and has Krypton-enhanced visionary powers but, Jesus, is he boring.

Turning again to the probable demographics of anybody reading this book, I am advised that it is likely you had some sort of tertiary education. Probably a college of some kind. So did I. I was a non-paying guest at Liverpool University for three years in the mid 1960s, sharing the city with at least a thousand wannabe Beatle groups. I did what I had to do to get my degree and, I guess, was a fairly routine student. Liverpool University campus is unique, possessing a Catholic cathedral at one end and an Anglican cathedral at the other. I visited neither during my stay. The student union bar was in the middle. I visited this place on most days. I played soccer at least four times a week. At the start of my final year, I was approached as I came out of the bar by a new student – who asked me where the University Library was. I had no idea. As I said, a fairly routine student.

Let's press the fast forward button from the 1960s to 1982. We beam ourselves, Star Trek-style, from Liverpool to the University of Texas at Austin. A clean-cut young man is arriving in a white BMW, which has been bought with the proceeds of a part-time job conducted before and after (and sometimes during and instead of) high school. The job was selling newspaper subscriptions, and earned him more in his last year of high school than his teachers took home. His success in selling subscriptions came from a simple idea – he saw that the highest demand for subscriptions came from newly married couples and/or people who had just acquired a house. Without going into too much detail, he found ways to target both those groups *directly*. A piece of a jigsaw makes its way into the box.

As he drove up to Austin, on the back seat of his car were three computers. Remember, this is an eighteen-year-old kid heading for college in 1982. If you could have moved me across the space-time continuum, on my back seat for that journey would have been two pairs of soccer boots, fifteen cases of beer, a carton of edible condoms (peppermint flavour), a tube of anti-acne cream, another tube of vile smelling embrocation which I used to rub on my legs before playing soccer (my theory was that if you weren't fit, you should *smell* fit), my music system, assorted records and tapes, enough sandwiches packed by my mother to last for three weeks and one pad of paper and a pen. The latter was an emergency kit in case I got confused and attended a lecture.

We've noted Dell's early direct-to-market thinking. I need to explain the three computers. Michael had been already been fascinated by numbers for over a decade, attending an advanced math class in junior high school and competing in math contests. In addition, he became increasingly interested in the technology surrounding numbers – and moved into the start of a lifelong (we assume!) love affair with computers and computing.

For his fifteenth birthday his parents bought him an Apple PC, and, with a mind already on the legend he was shortly to become, he gave commentating journalists the kind of lead-in story on which they thrive. He took the thing upstairs and took it apart. That, of course, is not the legend fodder. I could have done the taking-apart thing quite easily. That he was fifteen and *put it back together* is the milestone we want on the road to Nutterness. Another piece of the jigsaw takes vague shape.

If you and I had just stripped an Apple and reassembled it, I suspect we would have collapsed in some sort of *post-coital* trance on the bed. Not our Michael. He saw the opportunity that would lead him to build a business that would be three times the size of the aforementioned Apple within twenty years.

He began by upgrading computers. Moving from Apple to IBM-compatible PCs, he bought units as some people buy cars or houses – they then 'do them up' and sell them for a profit. They then repeat this, often increasing unit size and/or value and often until they die from being Sad Bastards. Michael did this with PCs, moving to buying upgrade parts in bulk before he left for college. He had three upgraded units in the back of the car when he got there (remember?). By now we know he is a blue-ribboned nerd, and another piece of the jigsaw tumbles into the box.

Now, I'm moving away from him for a while – because we need to look at what was going on in the commercial world of computers in a bit more depth.

You don't need me to tell you that the science and use of electronic data processing was growing at a phenomenal rate in the early 1980s. Frankly, if you want figures, you can go and find your own – they all make the same point and are all mind-boggling. What had been the exception rather than the rule a couple of decades previously was now emphatically the rule – and any company of size and stature by now possessed a computer room (or in some cases a computer centre) which was filed with mysterious looking blue fridges and manned by mysterious company employees who spoke a whole new language.

What is important for our story is that a trend within a trend was happening. For many in the wonderful world of computing, the science at that time was all about the central processing of massive amounts of corporate data and/or massive amounts of activities associated with that data. The benefits of computing were seen by many to be the automation of the basic company activities – payroll, bookkeeping, accounts payable and receivable, inventory control, production processing, sales data and blah-de-blah-de-blah. If computing were to reach the desks or workstations of corporate employees, it would be via remote terminal for these centrally processed functions. This was surely true in and of itself, and the resultant productivity benefits had already cost millions of blue collar and administrative employees' jobs. This trend would continue unabated, and millions more would pay the price for this historic hike in business effectiveness and efficiency. It's still going on.

Within that trend however, a sub-trend was already making its presence felt. It would grow to level where it would, arguably, at least rival the seminal trend in results and implications. It was the breakthrough that involved putting processing itself in the hands of the individual remote user. Along with specially designed operating systems and individualised software, we witnessed the advent of the PC.

Although it seems so obvious to us all now, few saw its full potential in the early 1980s. Indeed, it was that very myopia that almost brought IBM to its knees within a few years. There were, however, three forces at work, which set the wheels in motion – which would eventually revolutionise every aspect of out lives:

- First: chip technology was growing exponentially. It became possible to house adequate processing power within a desktop machine.
- Second: in parallel, individualised operating systems and custom-tailored software packages were beginning to allow that processing power to be harnessed at the desktop.
- A new market was emerging – to be known later as SOHO (Small Office, Home Office). As well as for individualised applications within big companies, the PC was starting to mine another rich seam of demand. The small business sector, already showing strong growth dynamics on the back of big company downsizing, found that a PC could not only help their productivity, but could make them look as professional in the market place as any of their big brothers. Irrespective of the benefits of processing accounts receivable by EDP, it is amazing what a difference is made in the imagery and stature of a small business if it sends out

an invoice that is printed on a professional document. In addition, many people were beginning to see the potential benefits of bringing one of these processing units home into the domestic arena.

A new market was in its genesis – the sale of PCs to individuals for use in specialised business situations or in the home. By the early 1980s two things were clear – that it was going to be a substantial market in its own right, and that *nobody knew how to sell to it*. The last part of that last sentence forms another piece of Michael's jigsaw.

At the start, PCs were treated more like TVs than cars – that is to say they were stacked on the shelves of the electronic goods retailers (along with microwaves, stereos, phones, vacuum cleaners etc.), rather than distributed to specialised authorised dealerships. In this way, the manufacturers sold in to the retailer, and the retailer sold on to the consumer – adding, as is retail habit, a margin for 'adding this value' which would often exceed fifty percent of the final retail price.

That retail mark up has traditionally reflected the fact that the retailer has to invest in real estate, a building, management and staff, control and information systems and the purchase of the inventory. That actually works well for a man who wants to buy a TV, as it enables him to wander into the store, stand and look at sixteen different models side by side, and have his wife decide which one they will buy. The user-important technology is not complex and it is relatively easy to see and understand the differences between models – some of which are simply cosmetic. It is, after all, a piece of furniture.

It would be nice to record, as a tribute to all those involved, that this was rapidly seen to be an inappropriate way of selling PCs to this emerging market, but that was not so. It seemed as though there was no other way, and all parties, with the exception of one, just plodded on. The evidence was there, however – the retailer was pocketing a big chunk of the added (monetary) value for very little value added to the supply chain.

From the customer's point of view, the retailer just didn't have the specialist knowledge, nor the necessary follow-up and service support, for this specialist product. This was *not* a TV or a microwave. The customers tended *either* to know very little, in which case an electronic-goods-store sales person who had only a superficial knowledge of the product specifications ('Er, this one is has a really nice sort of blue screen …') was no great help – a marriage of the unknowing buyer and the unknowledgeable seller. *Or*, the consumer knew a lot – in which case ditto. In general it was the latter as a very sophisticated consumer was emerging in this market. In addition, the sales support needed to be manufacturer specific as it had to include a helpline – so the normal retailer pitch ('The manufacturer's warranty is OK sir, but if you want *real* aftercare we suggest you take out our retailer-specific sales and service insurance cover, which happens to be run by our sister finance company … blah-de-blah-de-blah).

If all that wasn't bad enough, PCs were high-value items, and retailers are notoriously unhappy about keeping adequate stocks of such inventory, relying on a smoothie-sales person to convince you to buy from one showroom model, and then wait eight weeks for delivery. That was proving a frustration when specifications were changing with unprecedented rapidity.

So, the retailer wasn't cutting it for the consumer. Interestingly, the retailer was also proving to be a pain in the arse for the manufacturer as well. The producers had to gear up their sales forces to sell to the major retailing chains, which is, in and of itself, a specialist science. It is one of life's great experiences to try and peddle your wares to a major retail chain. Basically, you deal with something called Central Purchasing. You are treated like dog shit from the get-go, and the conversation centres entirely on retail-oriented variables. What is the latest possible stage the retailer has to acquire title to (aka pay for) the inventory, and is it possible that this stage can be

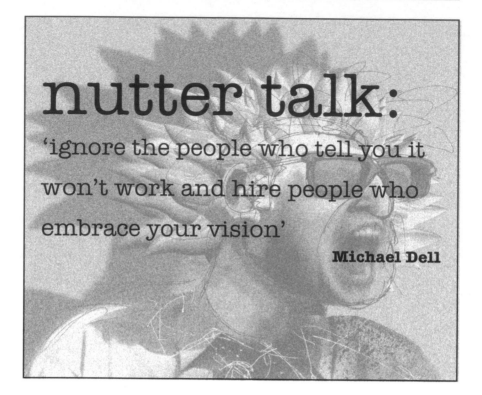

nutter talk:

'ignore the people who tell you it won't work and hire people who embrace your vision'

Michael Dell

preceded by the consumer having already bought it from the retailer? Never mind the details (e.g. processing size and speed) how can the wholesale price be kept down? Can special sales 'promotional' allowances be paid in cash direct to the retailer?

All this crap is what the PC manufacturer's specialist sales forces had to compete on. The areas in which they wanted to compete were quite different, of course – the sophisticated and constantly changing specifications and their specialised after-sales support.

The retailer was failing this supply chain in other ways. If a manufacturer sells to the consumer through a third-party retail link, it must produce against macro-forecasts. That's kinda easy if you manufacture Christmas cards, but in an early-stage market (like PCs in the 1980s) the only thing you can guarantee about your mid-term forecasts is that they will be WAY OUT.

In addition, the holding costs of – in this case high-value – inventory are high if you use retailers. You have to buy it to use it in the manufacturing process, then you produce it to hold it in your warehouse, then you transfer it to the retailers central warehouse, then some of it goes to the retail store and some of it gets delivered to the consumer. Eventually you get paid for it. This onerous process is bad enough if you are producing soap, but a new factor was emerging that made this sequence profoundly inappropriate for PCs. The science was changing almost daily. Processing speeds and capacity, operating systems and software applications were seeing breakthrough after breakthrough. If the manufacturer tied up inventory for too long, it was obsolete. Inventory in the PC world has been famously described as having the shelf life of lettuce.

I have used the last thousand words or so as practice – just in case I ever get a job as a journalist with the Sun newspaper. I have deliberately dumbed it all down into an amalgam of entry level Applied Economics and the *Beano*. I have done this for a reason – when you put it like that it seems like a collection of Statements of the Bleeding Obvious. I mean, even a Manchester United fan could have seen what was wrong and figured out the obvious thing to do about it. The retail link in the chain, which added a substantial portion of the end cost to a PC, was not adding any value, and may be subtracting it. Obvious, innit? You just cut 'em out. Sell straight to the end-user.

Oh, the benefits of hindsight. I was there. I was in my late thirties, relatively successful in big corporate life; I had a bit of money to invest and had a Wang PC on my desk. I shoulda-coulda seen it and become a squillionaire. But I didn't. Neither did you. Only one person saw it – one person with the background, the culture, the technical knowledge, the mind and the visionary powers (aka the needed jigsaw pieces) to put it all together and structure an entirely different supply chain.

Here are the three elements of his Nutty idea:

- He abandoned the retail link in the chain, and set up to deal directly with the end-user. From the outset this was not just a way of getting massed produced goods to the consumer, it was a relationship-based process. The consumer, ordering by phone or fax, could individualise the product. The 'sales force' were trained to deal with the needs of individual customers, not mighty retailers. Production was geared to the individual order, with the placed order following the PC through all stages of its manufacture. In short – the company formed a relationship with the individual, and the breakthrough moment for mass-customisation arrived.

- To compensate for the perceived concern of consumers who ordered an expensive product without the touchy-feely experience of holding it and seeing it, Dell offered a 30-day no-quibble guarantee. That solved *that* problem.

- Much has been written about how direct marketing improves the effectiveness and efficiency of inventory management. That's fine – to a point. Here's the *real* Nutty Idea behind this – Michael Dell makes your computer for you, *using your money.* Sure the inventory is minimised, sure it enables the latest technology to be applied, but the removal of the retailer's and the cash-flow benefits to the manufacturer meant that the consumer got a better product, better service and Dell could be ultra-competitive and ultra profitable.

The rest is history. Within four years of starting his business while attending college, Dell went public with a value of $59 million. Four years later Dell became one of the top five PC makers worldwide. Like many companies caught up in geometric growth, the very pursuit of maintaining it brings problems, and the core principles of his Nuttiness were abandoned around 1992–4, which saw the company lose some of its focus on the individual as a customer and go back into retail. All that did was hammer home how good the direct model was, and they recovered by going Nuts again.

The initial ways of relating to the individual – phone and fax – carried the business until the mid-1990s, when a tiny technical advance called the Internet began to stretch its wings. In 1996 Dell went on the Web, operating its Web site, www.dell.com. Today, more than $14 million Dell sales a day are processed through the site. Michael Dell's dream was already on fire, the Internet just put gasoline on it.

We have on our hands a Dream Merchant of the highest order. It was one thing to see that the retail link for the early PC market was a Leaning Tower Of Bullshit. It was quite another to put some special jigsaw pieces together that found an alternative – an alternative that has changed the face of modern business. In a couple of decades, mass marketing has almost been superseded by mass customisation. It took a Nutter to lead the way.

One of the factors that separate dreamers from Dream Merchants, in my observation, is the sustainability of the result. As the high-tech industry suffered in the early years of the new millennium, Dell's streamlined supply chain paid dividends. On average, the company carries about five days stock, compared to their competitor's range of 30–90 days. Their world is still about high-cost, depreciating assets. You wonder why the others didn't learn – indeed some, like Apple, indicate they are going the other way to respond to tightening markets, by setting up their own specialist retailing operations. I know which horse I'll back.

As we learn more of Michael Dell, the 'boring' label hangs about, but becomes irrelevant. What we also find is that he is a How-Boy of real stature as well. Obviously he has loosened his grip on the company, running the thing with a couple of powerful allies as part of the 'Office of the Chairman', but the company looks like him, tastes like him and smells like him. Like him, it is clean, efficient, focused and fearless. Its Nutterness – now institutionalised into widely accepted business practice – remains sacrosanct. It is still a relatively new company, and works in the world of wacky new PC technology – but its hair is tidy and it is rarely seen without wearing a tie. You know what I mean? Oh, he's a cool HowBoy all right.

NUTTER SCORE:

Dream Merchant: Five stars

HowBoy: Three stars

ANITA RODDICK

Hᴇʀᴇ'ꜱ ᴀɴᴏᴛʜᴇʀ ᴏɴᴇ ᴡʜᴇʀᴇ I will have to state my upfront prejudices. What's different here is that I think you should as well. Everybody, including her good self, has a view about this woman and 'her' Body Shop, and those views have a spectacular range.

It is not surprising that she and/or it have reached the parts other brands cannot reach. Although Body Shop 'only' has 1800 stores, it is halfway up the list of the world's fifty most-recognised brands. Rather like Benetton and Bill Clinton, few people have no opinion on the Body Shop and its founder.

Right, let's get these prejudices out of the way. Me first.

I am biased in favour of the woman. This is entirely spiritual and somewhat emotional. The reason would annoy her intensely, and has nothing to do with business. It's just that if the lighting is right, and you half close your eyes, she looks a bit like the dark-haired bird out of ABBA, and (purely in the interests of science) I need to declare that I was in love with her. In a Big Way. History does not, unfortunately, record her emotions towards me in return. So my love was unrequited, but that doesn't stop me wanting to sing 'Fernando' tenderly, in my rather pleasing tenor, every time I pass a Body Shop or see a photo of La Roddick.

This of course, is entirely sexist. As she points out, or rather yells, nobody passes judgement on what a guy looks like in business whereas every woman gets unconscious marks according to her appearance. Now, to this charge, I can plead innocence. I have dealt with many women in business, and she is the only one who looks *remotely* like the bird in ABBA. She is, therefore unique in my eyes, and you should know this. It should be disclosed. All other women I have met, however, have been judged as humans, just like the male of the species. I am colour-blind, gender-blind, disability-blind. I do not, however, enjoy the presence of smokers when they are partaking and, if anything, I am biased against some male appearances. Men wearing fob watch chains whilst sporting five grand's worth of Rolex on their left wrists annoy me, while those who have their initials embroidered on their shirts should be summarily shot.

Phew, that's *that* out of the way. Where was I? Where? Who? Oh, her.

Here's my second ongoing bias about her. Despite a lot of superficial evidence, I don't think we have a high-quality Dream Merchant here. But I suspect we might have an out-and-out HowBoy. Which, in the interests of equal opportunism, needs renaming as a HowGirl.

Now, that's my biases out of the way. Now, I'll leave a space, so you write down your biases about Roddick. Keep it tight, and *be honest*.

Exactly. I couldn't have put it better myself. My only comment on what you have written is that I don't think the letter 't' occurs twice in the word 'prat'. And you certainly don't spell sanctimonious like that. I think there is only one 'k' in it.

I confess my initial analysis seems hard to defend. If I quote Benetton as a blue-ribboned Dream Merchant, then *surely* there are echoes of how and why he got there when we consider Anita. After all, if he triggered his Nutterness with me with a powerfully nutty, billboard-based advertising campaign in the US, didn't Body Shop repeat almost the *exact* principle in almost exactly the same circumstances with their infamous 'Condom' advert in San Francisco? It was, quite simply, a jewel of controversial, high-impact, low-cost, cause-related advertising – although this time relying on words rather than Toscani's imagery. Responding to the growing Aids crisis, Body Shop hung a sign outside its high-profile San Francisco store that advised the world:

'2-4-6-8, USE A CONDOM OR MASTURBATE'

Only those readers who have had any experience of Big Brand ownership and management in the US (particularly if there are franchisees involved) can have any idea of the Hiroshima-style negative impact this kind of thing can have. The rest of you can just guess.

Hidden underneath the surface of America are vast reserves of humbug and millions and millions of what I can only pause, consider and then call religiously fundamental fuckwits. They all lie very near the surface, and the (perceived) science of brand management is that you can do ANYTHING but disturb them. If you are in the mainstream, and you even *hint* your brand accepts the existence of homosexuality (never mind hinting that you personally support it) it is like driving a small plane into a cliff face.

It really is hard to illustrate how strong a force is out there, but you can trust me when I tell you I faced this particular headwind personally many times. I have mentioned Burger King's launch of a $30 million campaign under the mischievous, amusing banner line: 'Sometimes You Gotta Break The Rules'. I noted how, within a couple of weeks, I had been *bombarded* by the religious right-wing, the Teamsters Union and the PTA of America – all yelling at me for leading the US off the straight and narrow. *And we never mentioned 'masturbate' once.*

You don't need me to tell you the response to the condom thing, but surely that supports Anita being levelled with Luciano as a Dream Merchant? Nope. And neither does her rhetoric, in support of such an elevation, count either. In her own book[1] she includes in her list of 'natural' entrepreneurial qualities:

> *'A touch of craziness … Crazy people see and feel things that others don't. An entrepreneur's* dream *[my emphasis] is often a kind of madness …'*

And *still* I stand by my position. Here's my reasoning. Anita Roddick is a hugely talented woman. She is also a Nutter by my definition. She had a dream all right, but that is not why she is in this book, and why the history of corporate life on earth (which will surely be filmed by David Attenborough one day) will accord her a page on her own. I believe the dream she had was flawed, and that disqualifies her from my Dream Merchant list. What's more, I don't think that dream was essential to what Anita Roddick's Nutterness achieved.

She could have done what she did had Body Shop been a chain of organic grocery shops, or shops selling only clothes made from natural cottons. Why she is here is not about what Body Shop does, but *how* she does what she does. Her considerable triumphs are based on her profound restlessness, and her deep beliefs on society, politics, people and life. *Body Shop was the bus she caught.*

In fairness, it is an original shape. The industry itself – cosmetics, perfumes and personal cleansing – is far from new. Evidence of self-decoration and the use of perfumed oils goes back way before

---

[1] *Business As Unusual*, Anita Roddick (Thorsons, 2000)

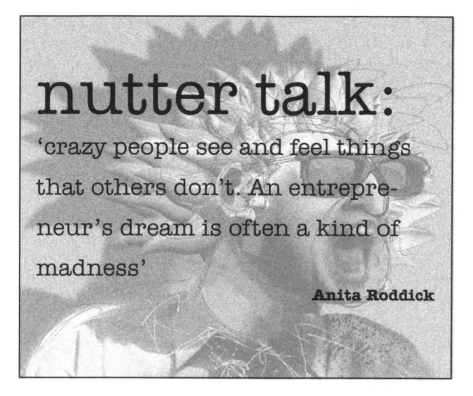

nutter talk:

'crazy people see and feel things that others don't. An entrepreneur's dream is often a kind of madness'

Anita Roddick

the Christian era. Frankincense was delivered to the young Christ in the manger. The use of scented soaps was well established in most European cities by the Middle Ages.[2]

The modern version of this industry took shape alongside the industrial revolution. As previously untold levels of personal wealth were created, so did the need to differentiate and pamper. The middle classes were created. To help the overall market receptiveness for Roddicks's ideas, one of the strongest market traits of all time – *the celebration of the small self-indulgence*[3] – was born around the time she began mixing her potions and dabbling in alchemy.

All this combined to transform the industry and give it its modern shape. Giant international corporations (Colgate-Palmolive,

---

[2] For some reason France must have missed out …
[3] The driving force behind Häagen-Dazs and Starbucks. Trust me.

Proctor & Gamble, Unilever) began mass production to satisfy the mass markets. Chanel, Revlon and Estée Lauder began to link some products with elitism and sexual allure. Department stores from Bloomingdale's to Boots began giving up more and more space to this industry – a level of space that now astounds the author every time he walks into (or rather rapidly through) one.

The beauty industry became the vertebrae of another one – advertising; with all forms of media (particularly print) generating substantial chunks of its advertising income from these products. Business management and brand management became seamless, and the economic model defied all convention. Margins were huge, and ploughed back into more elite marketing and front-of-store distribution. In many cases, if you put the price up, demand followed it.

During the 1970s, a number of existing economic models were being challenged. I had just joined Shell in the UK, and my job was to peddle motor oil to retail garages. If you wanted oil in your car in those days, it usually came via somebody checking your oil level as he or she filled up your car with petrol, and selling you a pint or two if you needed it. Other than that, it came via the garage as part of a maintenance service. It was, as we now know, sold at a ridiculously high margin.

I was paid a base salary, and I got points for selling oil into garages, which could be redeemed in a gift catalogue. I got wind, one day, of a guy who was in the market for oil, who wanted to sell it differently. He did indeed. My average wholesale was around six to ten cases. He bought a *truckload*. He planned to sell it retail, by the gallon, to motorists at such a price that they would see the error of their previous ways. They would ignore the garage, buy it themselves and put it in the car themselves. It was dramatically successful; so much so that a new supermarket on my patch, named Asda, called me in. They too wanted a truckload. I am still spending the catalogue points.

What the hell has this to do with skin lotion and cleansing cream? Everything. This revolution, from high-margin, motor oil products, delivered to the chattering classes at high prices on the back of superficial service and bogus quality claims, to 'pile 'em up and sell 'em cheap' was the one Body Shop brought, in parallel and in principle, to cosmetics. It ran like wildfire through many other sectors, changing the face of supermarket retailing and leading, eventually, to the concept of 'category killer' stores and whole-sale clubs. A large part of the world was saying: *'Cut the frills. Give us the same (branded) products, but take everything out of the price apart from the absolute basics of getting it in front of me'*.

The early Body Shop posed a similar challenge to the conventional economics of cosmetic retailing. The products were cheap. They were made cheaply, and passed on cheaply because there was little overhead. The concept was capitalised with a few grand, albeit aided by a lot of 'sweat equity'. There were no big advertising budgets. Er … there were no advertising budgets, period. The seminal decision to encourage a lot of package recycling seems to have been born of economic necessity rather than a conscious attempt to capture a smouldering consumer zeitgeist. The decision to use traditional materials seems to have been as much about getting small enough production runs for one outlet rather than a deliberate *volte face* from existing convention.

It is unfair, however, to simply lump Body Shop in with Kwik Save or Asda. The in-store imagery, and the product positioning and range, signalled something different from the get-go. By that, I mean from *before* the brand became associated with campaigning generally and Anita Roddick's campaigning specifically. Whatever the source of the green paint, the imagery of the early Body Shop brand is strong, clear and distinctive. The success of the first triggered a second store, and the decision to make them look the same was taken.

I do not believe this was a case of somebody assembling a handful of unique jigsaw bits into a picture – a Dream shape. It does not feel like the coming together of a personality, a mind, a set of circumstances and a range of skills that had been just waiting for the day they were joined together to provide an enduring and irreversible revolution in conventional business wisdom. In the first place, Body Shop evolved out of pragmatism. A profoundly – and I mean *profoundly* – talented woman needed to make a living, within certain restricting circumstances, while her husband was missing in action.[4] The Body Shop embryo was the result.

There is another reason why I do not rate this Dream shape as a true business epiphany. It has built-in flaws. It rapidly became a vehicle for Anita Roddick's beliefs on a whole range of issues – including many that were not just to do with her specific industry. Among those beliefs were deeply held convictions about the role and purpose of business itself in the modern world. Two, in particular, are consistent themes of hers. The first is that companies should play a much wider role as vehicles for social development and change. Their resources, size and impact in the world of globalism are such that they can and should play a role in the gap between the individual and government in everything from defending the environment to supporting human rights.

Her second consistent theme is linked, but different. Business should not measure itself just by conventional financial returns. She consistently wails that she wants the Body Shop to be good not big, and (from *Business as Unusual*), '*I would rather be measured by how I treat the weaker and frailer communities I trade with than by how big my profits are*'.

It may surprise you to know that, after thirty-plus years in big business, I have many sympathies with these views. Essentially, I quit big business because I was sick of failing basic tests of rightness every day. It is also my observation that these views, to a degree, are (a lot) more widely held than appears evident from scanning the business press. But here's my problem. Her quoted sentence above contains 24 words. Of those, three are 'I' and one is 'my'. In the Body Shop *she* is

---

[4] Gordon Roddick does not feature in this book, other than here. At this stage he was 'searching for his identity' or somesuch. If I ever write a book about guys who got lucky in marriage, he will be Chapter One. I will be Chapter Two.

the pilgrim and the company is the vehicle for *her* Pilgrim's Progress. This approach is fine while the company is yours and yours alone, but once you seek external financing, and once you seek to grow by franchising, then you encompass a conflict of interests within the brand that is like the San Andreas fault line – everything might seem fine and daily life goes on, but it's going to blow up one day.

These people, who are invariably asked to write big cheques to invest in one way or another in the company, usually have more conventional ways of seeking returns. At the very least it needs a rebalance of the corporate *raison d'être* to reflect that. It's all fine and dandy asking potential franchisees to write an essay rather than fill in a conventional application form, but they are investing. As are the stockholders. They may be a bit different from normal investors but, trust me, they don't want to further social causes *instead* of making a profit, they want to further social causes *as well as* making profit.

I had this problem with a music company in the US, who had sold 51% of the business to the public and asked me in as chairman. It took about a week for me to realise that, although the family had banked the money and technically owned or controlled the company, they saw no reason to change. I honestly don't think they *understood* that the family interests had to fall in the rankings, and that their primary roles were to defend the 'majority' interests of the true owners.

Anita Roddick has, of course, moved further away from the bridge of the good ship Body Shop, and is now nailed to the bow as a sort of masthead. That move was made partly by her, and partly by others with vested interests. She no longer steers the company, but remains the first thing you see or think about when Body Shop comes into view. This kind of conflict has erupted regularly within the castle walls of Body Shop. As I write, the latest yelling match is around the repurchase option the company gave to the American operator to buy the US operations. By cleverly issuing non-voting stock as part of the purchase, she has defended her Kitchen Cabinet's collective control of the company. She has also flipped a raised middle finger at the rest of Body Shop's investors. You can't keep doing that, and if she doesn't have the courage of her convictions to take it fully private again, she should get out. The alternative is a delayed, inevitable and damaging punch-up.

Don't get me wrong. Body Shop is a hell of an act, and she belongs in this company.

Cut through the rhetoric, add a teaspoon of cynicism, and today's Body Shop is a successful modern global brand which uses cause-related marketing more effectively and efficiently than any other. It is run by professionals who have done the 'right' things such as outsourcing production and blah-de-blah-de-blah. It looks strong in its sector and might be worth sticking a bit of your pension fund in.

Oh, and by the way, Body Shop, as a brand, can wheel out one of the most articulate spokespersons on the planet, and (in the same body) one of the world's highest profile emissaries and (in the same body), when needed, somebody who can institutionalise discomfort for us all. In a controlled, non-brand-damaging sort of way.

Why is she here? Quite simply, she is a HowGirl of the highest calibre. Top Drawer. Whether the cynical view prevails (the brand is using her) or the altruistic version gets the nod (she is using the brand) matters not. She was, is, and will remain what the brand stands for. Nobody is really interested in what Body Shop does (there are now many me-toos), but many are forced to notice *how* it goes about its business. That is all about Anita.

So, let's look at her HowGirl talents. In my observation, there are two groups of them. The first is all to do with *restlessness*. I confess, during two business-related degrees and about twenty years of my subsequent business career, I had never heard of, or seen, this word used to describe a talent. I heard it first from the mouth of my boss in GrandMet, when I asked him, some years after the event, why he picked me for Burger King. I had no knowledge of America, little of franchising and none of fast food. He told me the brand needed restlessness; it had been hibernating for too long and needed a period of frenetic activity. Since then, I have come to realise that without inbuilt restlessness, you and your business/brand fight with one arm behind your back. It is *the* necessary leadership skill *du jour*. Anita Roddick grows restlessness wild under her armpits. She harvests it fresh every day. She is tireless in the cause, and tireless in the search for new ways to manifest it. It is her restlessness that keeps Body Shop fresh, distinct and inspiring. If we are to learn anything from her model as a Nutter, it is about restlessness. Wannabe a new (business world) leader? Don't leave home without it.

She is, of course, more than just restless. Her second great strength as a HowGirl is her *conviction*. Some of her convictions are naive. I suspect if I had a pound for every time she has been let down by someone she trusted, I would be very rich. But she *believes* in things, she has an inbuilt sense of right and wrong, and she has a nose that can sniff out inequality and oppression two continents away. And when she believes in things, she cannot just sit in the grandstand and cheer them on from the cheap seats, which is what you and I do. She has to be on the field, pushing behind them, kicking the opposition, making it happen.

I am not going to list the causes with which Anita Shop or Body Roddick (they merge seamlessly at this juncture) have been associated. It would simply be filling space and if you have never heard of any of them you must have been enjoying a sabbatical on Jupiter. Some of these causes have been related to the cosmetics industry – such as decrying the use of animals for product testing and using products from oppressed and poor parts of the world (Trade Not Aid). Others have simply reflected political beliefs, such as support for GreenPeace and the extensive and high-profile campaign against the Nigerian government's (and, as it turned out, Shell's) abuses against the Ongoni tribe in pursuit of oil profits. There have been many others.

A century ago she would have been cast as a reformer, and I suspect would have been proud to be so. There is no such category in the early twenty-first century, as we seem to be under the impression that all the big reforming has been done. Which is a load of Imperial

Bollocks. The unprecedented wealth creation of the last century has still left too many rich people in poor countries and vice versa.

Anita Roddick is not Sting, babbling on about the rainforests while advertising Jaguar cars on TV. She is much more a John 'There is no wealth but life' Ruskin, seemingly born a century too late, but knowing there is more to do than ever. I can pay her no higher (personal) accolade than to say that I think the Body Roddick has become England's Liberal political party – that once clear and proud party for reform and enlightened thinking that has completely lost its way.

It has not been an easy journey, and a publicly-owned company is not a comfortable vehicle for her. The media have occasionally targeted her and/or the brand for attack – in particular on a couple of occasions where they used heat-seeking missiles. There has been internal combustion, with disgruntled franchisees, shareholders and senior executives losing the plot. But she and it have survived and thrived. However you define her role, her restlessness and conviction are still front-of-mind when anybody taps their own awareness of the brand that is called Body Shop.

Go on, half close your eyes. You can just see her face, can't you? It's none too clear, but that doesn't matter. Is that her singing? Listen carefully; you can just hear the words. C'mon, there's nobody listening. Forget your shyness and join me:

'If I had to do the same again, I would my friend, Fernando'

NUTTER SCORE:

Dream Merchant: Two stars

HowGirl: Five stars (plus two merits)

WALT DISNEY

5

IT TOOK A WHILE TO GET HERE, but we are now facing the Big One. The Daddy Of Them All. And we need to straighten out a few things before we dip even our toes in this pool.

The Disney that we know and some of you love is full of positive, happy, saintly characters, apart from EuroDisney in Paris, where all seven dwarves are called Grumpy in line with the rest of the population of northern France. Excluding that location, however, we can make that positive assumption for all the rest of the myriad Disney characters across the world. Their founder, however, was not like them. Nor has any other Disney person been that has crossed my path on the corporate side of this organisation – arguably trading under the world's most recognised brand name.

I have personally crossed swords with Disney teams twice. The first occasion was in the early 1990s, when I was on the bridge of the good ship Burger King. We stole in while our arch-rival (pun intended) was sleeping, and secured exclusive rights to the Disney name and products for promotional activities in the US retail hamburger sector. This is known in the US as the QSR business – as in Quick Service Restaurants. Whoever came up with that name obviously never lived through one of our lesser experiences in Burger King 'Drive-Thrus'. Yes, that is how *through* is spelled in many American retail establishments and, for the record: we had people *die* in there. But that's another story.

In fairness to McDonalds (who seemed asleep) and to ourselves (who saw something they didn't) the idea of promoting the sector to children by linking up with powerful kid-specific *different* brand names hadn't been exploited, and we recorded a huge success.[1] During the run up to the partnership, and less frequently when it was eventually up and running, I stared across a few tables in meetings with the Disney corporate team. Like most people on the planet, I knew of Walt Disney, I knew the bare bones of his story – but had never come remotely close to meeting him. These guys, the corporate fruit of the loins of the great man, left me feeling flat – for the simple reason they were *no* different to the rest of executive America. They were pleasant enough to deal with on the surface. Underneath they were the usual Suits – no more, no less.

Five years after leaving Big Business, I arm-wrestled with corporate Disney again – this time on a different level. I was (still am) co-founder of a retail service concept that mixes a restaurant and a theatre – which we christened *Y Arriba Y Arriba*. The more cosmopolitan of you will have figured out the Latin connection here – it

---

[1] We simply twinned up with Disney's summer or holiday movie, and offered Disney merchandise linked with the movie either free of charge with a kid's meal or for a small premium price. The success with such as *The Lion King* was astonishing – so much so that McDonalds 'bought' the sector back after I had left BK. I understand the buy-back price they were forced to pay was mouth-watering. HeeHee!!!!

serves *tapas* dishes from each of the 21 Latin countries while Latin-themed entertainment goes on all around the *café-teatro*. Although it was new, and we were a new company, and Disney normally won't touch a partnership with either, they made an exception on both counts because they didn't have a Latin concept for their massive expansion of the original Disneyland. They heard of us, we got into discussions and we ended up negotiating a lease. We opened the first one at the Anaheim site early in 2001. Have you ever negotiated a lease with Disney people, and then tried to work it? It's roughly the same as putting your nipples in an iron vice and having somebody tighten it while Kenny G plays pap in the background.

Those two stories merit a book in their own right, but not this one. The purpose of including them is to make the point that, despite the zillions of dollars sunk into the Disney brand equity, and the sunshine and smiles imagery, it is not difficult, to slightly misquote P.G. Wodehouse, to distinguish between a senior Disney corporate executive and a ray of sunshine.

The immediate conclusion is that modern Disney executives have betrayed his heritage, but an hour of research will point you at the inescapable conclusion that the great man himself did not bottle his own persona and peddle it to the world via the smiles of Mickey Mouse and the innocence of Snow White. He did not source his dream by looking in the mirror and letting the world in on his lifestyle and life rules. Quoted in Bob Thomas's biography of his brother Roy, Walt himself is quite clear on what he didn't personally contribute to the dream:

> *'I've worked my whole life to create the image of what Walt Disney is. It's not me. I smoke, and I drink, and all the things we don't want the public to think about'*

Neither was he, counter to popular legend, the greatest animator/artist ever. His technique simply was not of the required quality – and he rapidly delegated that side of the business to better artists.

In short – he was not a HowBoy. The Dream wasn't him, but it was his. And now it starts getting a bit complicated. Here is the first real example – in this book and, I think, on record – of somebody who created a dream not just because it was right at the edge of what was physically possible. He did that without a doubt – and that, alone, might have been achievement enough to chisel him onto any memorial stone. But his dreams involved more than just doing something nobody had done before – they involved being able to see around corners. He created dreams to satisfy customer trends that hadn't yet appeared at the time he created the dream. One example: he didn't create a theme park as a end in itself. He foresaw the explosion in the growth of travel and tourism – and provided product for it.

Let me expound a strange theory. You can pass a pleasant half hour in any company arguing about his greatest achievement. There is a whole range to ponder – my own favourite being his production of the first full-length (or 'feature-film' length) cartoon. My contribution to the debate is powerful: I draw an analogy with my beloved soccer. As you may know,[2] a soccer game lasts 90 minutes. Now, imagine the response if you took the following crazy idea to the appropriate authorities. Let's assume you had already led one great breakthrough in the game by championing the move from black and white into colour, and now you are following up with another winning idea. Or, as Baldrick might describe it to Blackadder – a really cunning plan. Instead of 90 minutes, you wanted to extend the duration of a single game of soccer to *fifteen hours*.

Can you imagine the response? There would be cries of 'Nonsense' and 'Idiot' somewhere in it, you may be assured. On a bad day you might be called a Silly Tosser. But that is a precise analogy of what Walt Disney proposed when he had the idea to do his full-length animated cartoon, *Snow White and the Seven Dwarves*. He would turn the existing eight-minute format into a full-length

---

[2] Well, if you are an American, maybe you don't. Soccer is that strange sport the rest of the world plays, and when it has a 'World Cup' it involves more than one country.

feature film. He did so in 1937, and the rest is history – but few, even now, realise how profoundly different (and risky) it all was.

So, you pays your money and you takes your choice – what was his biggest achievement? *Snow White*? *Fantasia*? Disneyland? For me, it's none of the above – or any of the other huge range of characters, facilities, events, products and merchandise that trade under the Disney brand badge. For me, this immortal Dreamer goes down in history for anticipating three of the great demand trends of the last century, and to do them justice I'm going to change fonts and list them:

- **Television**
- **Travel & Tourism**
- **Product**

The last one will help me explain. I can already hear yells of 'Resign' and 'Total Bollocks' coming from some of you. Product? Didn't the first caveman who made a clay bowl and swap it for some animal skins make a product? Didn't the guys at Coca-Cola make that product before Disney was alive? Didn't Ford have a range of products well before *Snow White*? All those statements are true, and they are all as may be. But I didn't say 'a' product, or 'the' product, or even 'some' products. I said product, which is a complex modern business phenomenon, neither singular nor plural and not requiring any definitive article. As a concept, it is best understood by us becoming a flies on the wall of a couple of mythical boardrooms i.e.

Example 1: The chairman speaks

> *'Guys, listen, and listen good. We have just acquired a cable TV channel. We now own four of them, plus several newspapers. That's 300 TV hours and about a mile of column inches we have to fill each week. What we need now is PRODUCT, OK? We need STUFF to put on there.*

Example 2: The chairman speaks

> *'Guys, listen and listen good. Our hamburger chain is about to enter the summer trading period. There are two things we all know about this period. First, the kids are off school. Second, THEY choose where the family eats when they are out together. Now, we all know they don't give a HOOT about our food or anybody else's. They make their – sorry, the family's – decision based on which chain has the best freebie toys or gismos that come with the meal. Guys, we need product. We need STUFF to give 'em other than food.*

Walt Disney saw these trends – television, travel and tourism, and the demand for product – WAY before any of his peers, and shaped his dreams to be ready for them when they arrived. That was his genius.

Let's start with television. In 1936, when television was still a million miles away from being a part of everyday and everyone's culture, Walt Disney was renewing his cartoon distribution contract with United Artists. UA insisted on owning the rights for some new fangled thing called television. Now remember, Disney was still a relatively young company. It had only been ten years previously that the three magic words 'Walt Disney Studio' appeared on a one story white stucco building, in a sixty-by-forty-foot lot at 2719 Hyperion Avenue in Los Angeles. Those first ten years were not easy, with every small success being offset with a setback or let down. In 1936 they were still short of cash and TV was not to become a public medium of any consequence for many years. Astonishingly, Disney refused to sign away TV rights, and left UA as a result. That's prescience with a capital P. It's the kind of decision that I still find amazing, being involved, as I am now, with a couple of new companies that are always hungry for burn-rate cash.

I am telling you now that I, along with 99.9% of entrepreneurs I know or know of, would have sold the TV rights in 1936 and banked the cash at that time and in those circumstances. His brother Roy, the financial anchor of the fledgling enterprise, wanted to. Not for the first (or last) time, Roy lost out to his creative but bloody-minded brother.

Just what the hell did this man, a producer of animated cartoons, see in the future of television that no-one else could – other than a handful of 1930s techno-geeks?

Disney's recognition of the future opportunities offered by TV was emphasised further in 1953 when Walt became the first (film) studio head to form an alliance with a TV company – in this case the ailing ABC. The deal stunned Hollywood – after all, TV was the enemy of the traditional film studios. Not to a Dream Merchant of his calibre, it wasn't.

Part of the deal was that ABC helped fund the capital for Disneyland, and many commentators file the deal as a piece of financial pragmatism – sourcing funds for something the banks wouldn't touch. I think not. My observation is that it was of at least equal importance to him to get Disney into America's front rooms and constantly in the face of America's families. First America, then the world.

The ABC-Disney partnership proved fruitful for both sides. Disneyland, the show, gave ABC ratings it had never had, and led to more shows. Eventually, it was to end in bitterness, but the point to remember here is that its genesis was not in 1953, but in the mind of a genuine Dream Merchant back in 1936.

The mid 1950s also saw the debut of what many see as Walt's most visionary dream-come-true: Disneyland.

Who knows quite when this idea formed in his mind. Amusement parks already existed in the 1950s, and Walt, once he had a broad concept in mind, researched many of them in the first couple of years of that decade. What is more interesting for my thesis is that this research also included visits to tourist centres. The dirt and litter of the amusement parks certainly led him to believe he could do something on a quite different plane of quality, but it is plain that this was never just a neighbourhood amusement park in his imagination.

Again, the project was born with the wind in its face. In the early fifties Disney was deep in debt to Bank of America, and no conventional investor would touch it. Eventually, armed with ABC's line of credit, the Disneys bought 270 acres in Anaheim, about 25 miles south of the expanding Los Angeles. The year was 1954, and they paid $4500 an acre[3] for the plot. The first orange tree was cleared in August of that year, with the opening promised an astonishing eleven months later. The costs rocketed from $4.5 million to an eventual $17 million, and nearly broke the company. It did, temporarily, smash the close working and filial relationship previously enjoyed by Walt and Roy, but the former never wavered. He was prepared to pay any price to get this particular boat away from the dock.

Now, here's where I differ from the majority of commentators on this amazing piece of history and dream-delivery. Of course Walt was committed to its content. He knew every detail of every piece of construction, and seems to have overseen the assembly of most of it. Of course it was a creative and 'imagineering' breakthrough. It remains my belief, however, that what Walt really saw, when he closed his eyes, was the explosion in the travel and tourism industry, not a bunch of rides and man-made towers.

As a definitive Boomer, my first personal memories are of those early 1950s. I was, of course, in England – spiritually, climactically and economically a long, *long*, way away from southern California. But we were becoming aware of a different way of life. We still had rationing, and our primary industries were accelerating their terminal decline, but there was a sense of optimism abroad, and within a decade the Prime Minister of the day, Harold McMillan, felt comfortable in telling us that we had never had it so good. They proved to be the only memorable words he ever uttered.

---

[3] In the late 1990s the going price for adjacent land was $2 million an acre. If nothing else, Disney's investment must look good at balance sheet revaluation time.

nutter talk:

'Disney's land: dream and diversify, and never miss an angle'

Wall Street Journal

Across the Atlantic, despite the shadow of Korea, the US began its new-ish role of world economic and political superpower with a confidence that reflected back from the mirrors of the majority of its population.

The lower-middle and working classes of both countries began to have substantial discretionary spending power – albeit on a different scale in the two countries. Travel by road, rail and (increasingly) air began to feature more and more as part of the personal leisure mix. Increasingly, real-time media illustrated exciting new places and different ways of living. Thanksgiving day in the US and Boxing day in the UK began to see a new 'tradition' being observed – that of gathering around a table and planning the family vacation. I am convinced it is this that Disney saw. A vision of people with money in their pockets, leisure time on their hands, the wherewithal to travel and a need for family destinations. Disneyland was his way of providing one-stop shopping to meet that demand.

Now for the one that fascinates me – the dream called Product. Again, an early clue is there for all to see, and again, we only see it with the benefit of magnified hindsight. In 1930, the Disney brothers were locked in a dispute with parties who distributed their cartoons. As part of a settlement that enabled him to move to another distributor, Walt agreed to pay a 'ransom' of $100,000 to regain the rights to his first twenty three (short) movies. Around the same time, he suffered the defection of his main animator to a rival. A simple decision was taken: never again would the Disneys lose control of their product. The difficulty I encountered in my two late-century dealings with Disney's modern day cavalry is only partly down to the fact that they were charisma-inhibited Suits. It also reflected that the company manifests the strongest brand governance on the planet – and there can be no doubt where the genes of this approach to business life came from.

Around the same time as the decision to retain control of everything possible to do with their name was taken, another event triggered a corporate development that now probably bugs most parents as they are dragged for a family meal into McDonalds *et al*. After the initial success of Mickey Mouse, Walt was pestered by a guy who wanted to put the mouse's image on cheap writing tablets. Predictably, it went wrong, and a short, sharp lawsuit stopped the guy in his tracks. The brothers learned two lessons. First: it opened their eyes to the potential of merchandising. Second: it drove home again the need to own and control the name and content of anything to do with their brand. In 1930 they signed a contract with a New York company for the making of toys and other objects with the likeness of Mickey and Minnie Mouse. The actual date was February 3, 1930. It is important. It signals the birth of Product.

The lawsuit preceding the signing of that contract also gave evidence of a style of brand and product management that remains evident today. When they, as plaintiffs, hit the defendant, they didn't seek a monetary remedy. Their primary goal was simple – to get him to stop what he was doing. Their second, subsidiary, goal was to turn the guy around – to get him to become a *legal* agent for Disney product. It is a *modus operandi* that still exists in Burbank today.[4]

Toys were followed by comic strips. Comic strips were followed by, well, you name it. The US was followed by the rest of the world. The rest of the story is, as they say, history.

It is estimated that, in 'developed' western society, the average human is now exposed, in one form or another, to at least 3000 brand 'messages' a day. It is hard to believe that such a figure will not include a gaggle of Disney exposures. I have not seen or heard of a figure reflecting the extent of a modern consumer's exposure to Product. I tried to figure it out based on my own lifestyle, but gave up exhausted when the total reached seven figures. By which time I had almost finished my breakfast.

Disney's ownership of Product ranks somewhere between 'Scary' and 'Terrifying'. It would probably be impossible to take a full and accurate inventory. The *tapas-teatro* I mentioned at the start of this chapter, now open in Disneyland, Anaheim (plug, plug) has no Disney name on it. To them, however, it is Product. Product is like bindweed taking over the world's garden. I hope that, after this short essay, there's a chance you may now recognise it. If you do, you know the *exact* day it was created.

Television. Travel and tourism. Product. These were his dreams. They became fundamental trends of the twentieth century, and there is overwhelming evidence he saw them in pre-natal form. His vision of all of them was clear enough for him to respond in advance. He marshalled his resources – his creative genius, his opposite pole of a brother, his characters, his agreements, his *everything*, and as the world discovered its demand for the three exciting new ways of life, he was already in shape on the supply side.

---

[4] Disney's corporate HQ. It is strangely un-magical, particularly if you are trying to park your car.

If there has been a better Dream Merchant, he or she has avoided my search.

NUTTER SCORE:

Dream Merchant: Five stars (plus double merit)

HowBoy: One star

STEVE CASE

6

EPENDING ON WHERE YOU GOT IT FROM, and depending also on whether my publishers got their act together, there is a good chance you are reading this book before the year 2003.[1] In which case, I would like you to pause and consider two remarkable facts:

- less than a *decade* ago, there was virtually no World Wide Web (www); and
- less than a *decade* ago, there was virtually no commercial Internet.

---

[1] There is a chance, of course, that you are reading this in the year 3005 as part of the contents of a recently opened time capsule. In which case, will you please raise a spiritual cheer for my soccer team (Manchester City) who are playing a team from Neptune in the Inter-Galactic Champions League tomorrow. I knew success would come one day …

Can you believe it? Has any technical development ever had such an impact so quickly? I think not.

I will add a third mind-boggler, largely for my own amazement. It was in October 1989 that it was finally confirmed that I would be appointed to head the Burger King corporation in Miami, subject of course to the success of my parent company's acquisition of the Pillsbury Group. My parent company was GrandMet, and Burger King nestled unhappily in the Pillsbury Empire. As I write this, it seems twelve years have passed since then – the tiniest of pin-pricks[2] in the history of commerce, let alone mankind. Yet it was only then, *in that same month*, that a deceptively shy, rather boyish-looking entrepreneur called Steve Case incorporated a company called America Online.

Since then, the Web and the commercial Internet have grown to an extent that is beyond the comprehension of most mortals. In parallel, and itself catalytic to the growth of the Web, America Online (AOL) has also grown to a level, and at a rate, which defies belief. Prior to the 'marriage' with Time Warner, less than a decade after its genesis, AOL's market value exceeded that of Coca-Cola. In the seven years from 1993–97, AOL subscribing memberships rose from 300,000 to *thirty million*.

Wow. So Steve Case makes my list of Dreamers and/or How-Boys with room to spare. And we must, surely, create a category for him that is dedicated to Dreamers Who Dream Huge Dreams Which Arrive At Breakneck Speed. We might even classify him as The Guy With The Biggest Dream Which Arrived The Fastest. We could, but we won't – because I fear that doesn't do him justice.

He is a Dream Merchant, but there are two aspects to his Dream that form better category titles for our purposes. I'll dive into both of them in a couple of minutes, but let me summarise them here first because I want to make a couple of pre-qualifying points. I'm going

---

[2] Remember, in Europe, it can take a century to get a *lawn* in acceptable shape.

to call the first category *The Dream Borne Out of Continuous Adversity*. The second will have an even longer name. I've tried to edit it down, but the best I can do at present is to call it *The Dream Borne out of Using the Most COMPLEX Technology to Make Life SIMPLE for the Customer*.

When I've done those two, I'm going to make the case for him as a better-than-average HowBoy. That cherubic exterior hides a bit of a Nutter. A very effective Nutter.

I'll get on to those in a minute. Let me first digress away from Steve Case and AOL. If we are analysing Dream Merchants and HowBoys, then it is right that we should wade through a list of those who exemplify success at either or both. It is also useful, on occasion, to look at the opposite – at organisations and/or people who had a Dream plonked in their hands – and who then lost it. We can learn from both.

In 1960 Theodore ('Ted') Levitt, writing in the *HBR*,[3] explained how and why the kerosene oil industry almost died at the beginning of the twentieth century. Kerosene was, at the time, along with gas, the main source of fuel for the world's lighting. The oil companies consequently focussed on beating gas and improving kerosene's inherent lighting characteristics. In short – the oil industry leaders assumed they were in the kerosene industry. They were good at what they did, and assumed the future looked good. Within a decade or two, however, kerosene was all but wiped out as a light source in the developed world. The impossible had happened – Edison invented a light that used neither oil nor gas.

Levitt's thesis is that had the oil industry guys assumed they were in the *illumination* industry rather than the kerosene industry, they (and not somebody from outside) would have invented electricity. Levitt then applies the same analysis to the mortal wounding of the railways and movies.

In the early 1990s it was becoming clear that the science and art of communicating was on the verge of some spectacular develop-

---

[3] 'Marketing Myopia', Theodore Levitt, *Harvard Business Review*, 1960.

ments – even if only a handful of nerds (and Steve Case) had any idea of how this might manifest itself. There were two parties in particular who were in pole position to be at the vanguard of such a movement, who could have developed themselves and the industry and played the sort of catalytic role that AOL ended up playing. Those were the postal services and telecommunications companies of the developed nations. AOL.com *should* have ended up being called something like USPS.com or GPO.com, or AT&T.com or BT.com. Indeed, some of those do exist today – but they are many dollars short and many dollars too late.

In hindsight, the telecoms giants and the postal services companies acted and thought in the same way the kerosene myopics did a century earlier. They assumed they were in the postal industry and telephone business. They were not. They were (are) in the communications industry. They were leaders in it, and it was them who should have lead the way. If we are trying to understand how Dream Merchants win, it helps sometimes to see how plonkers lose.

One more precursor on AOL. I'm going to declare my interests. I am a user and a fan. I am also a Boomer, and of a generation who were almost (I repeat, *almost*) overcome by advances in personal technology. Most of the generation behind me opted out of even trying to adapt to the changes. Most of the generation after me treat the most advanced technology as though they were cleaning their teeth with it. It is part of daily life and no big deal. My generation bridged the gap, and most of us did it reluctantly, slowly and quite badly.

I began using online technology while at my desk as the CEO of Burger King in, I think, 1992. We had IBM systems, and I wanted to lead our business, which was rather Luddite and conservative, into a new dawn – using value-adding high technology where possible. I was trained in the use of my PC and gave it a good shot. Sears and IBM jointly owned Prodigy, one of the Internet service providers available at the time – and I was duly instructed in its use and application. After my first lesson, I found I had no real need, and absolutely no enthusiasm, to use it further.

A couple of years later, after I had left big business, an AOL free disc came through my letterbox, and I loaded it on my PC. I've been a user ever since. Sometimes, it is true, I have been annoyed and frustrated, but I've stayed with them. Here's the prime reason for my loyalty, and it is so SO basic. I need the agent for my access to the Internet to *make it easy for me*. So, in my observation, do the vast majority of my generation – and I suspect we form a big chunk of the market growth achieved by AOL in the mid-to-late 1990s. Interestingly, when I repatriated to the UK recently, I compared six service providers, as I had to stop using the US based AOL server. After comparison, I 'switched' to AOL UK. Still the same reasons – the price is good and they make it S-O-O-O-O user-friendly. It is my observation that AOL's ability to appeal to users like me was a critical success factor in their growth.

Now, let's look at the chemistry of the Dream, and we'll start in a strange place. About a decade ago, I was invited up to Pittsburgh by the city bigwigs to be part of an evening's tribute to Tony O'Reilly – sometime Irish Rugby international, sometime creator of Kerrygold butter but more recently chairman of the Pittsburgh-based Heinz business empire. I shared the top table with him, and I think I presented him with his mini-Oscar as a memento of the occasion. Americans do this kind of thing so well, but it is faintly discomforting to Europeans so I got a bit pissed and can't remember too much about it all. Apart from his speech, that is.

After all the videos, tributes and presentations, the Great Man got up to give a short speech, and if you've never been in a room when he has done so you have missed something special. His delivery was magic, his subject fascinated me. He spoke of his admiration of the American people. He recounted his theory on how most nations are borne of victory, as Nation A rolls over Nation B, usually as a result of war. Most national cultures, therefore, are created by victors – but this was not so in the case of the USA. To a great extent, the US was created out of adversity – as refugees fled conquerors and/or oppressors and/or hard times in their homelands.

His conclusion was that the US has a unique heritage of defeat and adversity – and as a result an inbuilt sensitivity for the suffering of fellow human beings. If you take a deep breath and set aside the historic treatment of native Americans and African-Americans, and loosely file that under 'another time, another place'[4] – then I agree with him. His main conclusion, however, was about the *result* of the heritage of adversity. In fact, far from creating a weak nation, it has created a nation of unique strengths.

There is something about Steve Case and AOL that echoes this story. In a similar vein, I marvelled at the sight of Keith Richards on a recent television interview. He is, by technical definition, alive – but he shouldn't be. It is true, I suspect, that he has evolved into some carbon-based life form that now requires careful and thoughtful study, but he has survived everything that life as a rock star could throw at him, and he still commands a huge following with an increasingly doddery old band.

Similarly, during my time living in Miami, I came across cockroaches of a size that should have been required to file flight plans before they set off on a journey. I used to SMASH them, but they'd just lie stunned for twenty seconds, and then get up, stick their arms back on and carry on doing whatever it is cockroaches do. If possible, they looked even more determined.

Steve Case owes something to the Keith Richards/cockroach school of Dream Merchants. After what he has been through, he should be dead in the water, but he survived. He and his company are stronger for the journey.

I'm not going to expand much on the frequent and sequential snapping-off of assorted arms and legs of AOL on its short journey.

---

[4] We don't want to get too critical here. Not many 'developed' nations can look back on the last couple of centuries with a clean humanitarian record. Whenever I am tempted to mount a high horse on this subject, I force myself to remember it was Britain who invented concentration camps.

They've been written about elsewhere, and they are fascinating in their own right. I'm just going to list them with some summary explanations and background – because what I want to illustrate are the *dynamics* of AOL's decade of adversity. I want to try and show just how fast and furiously the ambushes came at Case – and then how he dealt with them, while never losing faith in the Dream. All this was instrumental in his success.

To start with it should be remembered that AOL, when it was incorporated as such, was itself born out of failure. During the 1980s, it began life as a pre-natal version of Napster and the music downloading/MP3 buccaneers that arrived fifteen years later. Home Music Store Inc. offered a service whereby, via a Neanderthal modem, PC users could listen to, and record, previews of popular music. The plan was then that HMS would sell them the records at a discount. It hit the same wall, for the same paranoid reasons, as the downloaders did later on.

HMC then morphed into Control Video Corp, offering video games on line. Case was rising in the company through this time, and enthusiastically played his part in spending $9 million dollars on selling 2400 Gameline modules. As somebody helpfully pointed out, they could have sold more off the back of a truck. But as somebody else wisely put it – the pile of horseshit they had was so big, there might just be a pony buried in it somewhere. If there was, it was becoming clear it would look like the online technology championed by Steve Case.

A third entity was born in 1985 – Quantum Computer Services Inc. It offered an online access and service called Q-Link – and tied in directly with PC suppliers, first with Commodore (who simply couldn't or wouldn't perform as a rainmaker) and then Apple. The relationship with the latter descended into a pissing contest, and Apple bought them out in 1989. The $2.5 million it paid was much needed. In 1989 Quantum had lost nearly $6 million, had blown millions in investment capital and had less that $1 million left. It was, however, 'free' to start its 'proper' role in life as America Online. To use an Americanism to summarise Case's start position; he was already batting 0 for 3.

Enemies are adversaries – and AOL began life facing two that should have destroyed it while it was still staggering around on wobbly legs. CompuServe was a specialist online service, wholly owned by HR Block, the giant, rather conservative mid-western US tax-preparation company. It was seen as a channel of trade that would eventually support HRB's mainline business, but it had huge resources behind it and could – and should – have taken and held pole position in the fledgling industry. Parent company conservatism proved its undoing.

In broad parallel, two mighty forces combined to form another online access service called Prodigy. Sears and IBM spent $500 million to launch it – and you may be old enough to remember when $500 million was a lot of money. It was the spiritual opposite of CompuServe: bright and breezy and funky, or so it told itself. Essentially, it was focussed on selling merchandise, and from the outset seemed to capture everything Sears knew about IT and everything IBM knew about retailing. Nevertheless, it boasted 500,000 subscribers within weeks of being launched.

In retrospect, AOL was like a turtle egg hatching, with its precarious first scuttle to the safety of the sea vulnerable to two giant predators. It survived, partly *because* it wasn't a giant – and in a fast moving new science could respond quickly whereas the others were sluggish. Nor was it focussed on the vested interests of parents like the two Biggies were – it was focussed on the demand side of the equation.

Those two factors provided enough covering fire to get AOL established. A third predatory competitor was to emerge, however, and it was one that would dwarf any threat that CompuServe or Prodigy, whether separate or together, could mount. It would also be far harder to deal with. It didn't look very terrifying because it wore spectacles. It came from Redmond, near Seattle. The monster's name was Microsoft, a huge ugly animal ridden by Bill Gates.

A mix of Case's surefootedness and the missteps of its two big competitors saw AOL progress rapidly in the first three years of the nineties – reaching one million members in 1993. In a meeting during that year Gates famously told Case that he could see three options for Microsoft to make its move into cyberspace. Option one: it could buy part of AOL. Option number two: it could buy it all. Lastly, it could enter the business itself and BURY AOL. Case cheerfully told him the first two were not an option, and that he should go and buy a shovel if he wanted to try the third (or something like that). I suspect his heart was pounding a bit when he communicated his response. AOL's prospects were promptly written off by sector commentators.

Several pairs of eyes continued to watch AOL's progress from Fortress Microsoft and, late in 1994, Bill Gates announced his Big Burial Move. MSN, Microsoft's very own Internet Service Provider (ISP) was launched, and the intention announced that it would be 'bundled' together with the soon-to-be-introduced Windows 95 operating system. Ouch. The vultures gathered again, preparing to dine on the carrion of AOL.

It didn't happen. As it happens, David beat Goliath. Again, let me stress that this is not an historic commentary on the details of this stuff – I just want to skim the rooftops so that you can *count* the setbacks that AOL faced – and get a feel for the scale of them. Case fought off the Microsoft threat, using three tactics. He continued his 'saturation bombing' of the market to increase awareness and trial of the 'brand' called AOL. Second: he used his hot stock value for a series of corporate acquisitions to goose the content of, and services provided by, AOL. Finally – he (very cleverly) fanned the anti-trust flames that were already lapping the ankles of the Redmond giant.

The latter tactic was a 'beaut' as the Australians might say. Coining the immortal phrase that Microsoft was becoming the 'dialling tone' of the PC world, and adding some epoch-making sound bites such as FG8S,[5] Case did enough damage to cause MSN to fumble its own launch. At the time I am writing this, MSN still only has

---

[5] If you are into text messaging you won't need a translation. If not … it stands for 'Fuck Gates'.

five million members – weighing in at about one-sixth the size of AOL. David didn't kill Goliath, he just reversed their roles. MSN never recovered, but this phase of the AOL/MSN spat only ended a battle. The war with Microsoft was not finished, it is still not finished, and may not be for a long time.

The short-term victory over the MSN monster saw AOL, battered but alive, stagger into the mid-nineties. Just when it appeared safe to go back in the water, however, the growth-mad Case and his company were hit by a series of blows in rapid succession.

The first came in the form of a relatively new market symptom called 'Churn', whereby customers hooked up with an ISP on the back of an 'unbeatable' introductory offer, and then left when it expired and/or a better one came along. Churn reached epidemic proportions in the ISP industry, and AOL, as its emerging leader, took the biggest kick on the tenderest knee. Suddenly, it seemed that industry growth was built on its own San Andreas fault.

Next, a professional general manager, brought in to AOL to appease Wall Street, departed after four months. Then, the ubiquitous Case had an affair with one of his senior managers, the only good news being that she was female. He promptly sold a bundle of his personally owned company stock to pay for his divorce, and you know how Wall Street always *loves* that.

As if all that wasn't enough, dubious accounting practices were exposed, and AOL proformas had to be restated in a way that wiped out every profit that AOL had ever booked. Minor Earnings Per Share (EPS) surpluses that had been booked were 'adjusted' to losses of nearly four dollars per share.

You get the picture? You've heard nothing yet. All that lot proved to be minor compared to what happened next. By 1996 customer expectations were changing in the world of ISPs. Unlimited use for a fixed price was beginning to appear, and it highlighted not only AOL's refusal to follow that route, but some dubious 'rounding up' of the metered usage in their existing way of doing things. In the end AOL had no choice, and it was forced to lay what became known in the circles of the ISP world as the Big Turd. It introduced fixed-price, unlimited-use billing. Chaos ensued. Their systems suddenly found themselves trying to drink from a fire hose as an unprecedented increase in usage brought huge (and I mean HUGE) access problems. These service problems themselves came hotfoot after a near 24-hour system crash. AOL was forced into a programme of customer refunds. Investors seemed as impressed as consumers – the stock price of the company dropped by two-thirds.

Pause with me for a minute. Do you remember the movie of Mohammed Ali being pounded by Joe Frazier? Backed up on the ropes, he held his defences high, and let Frazier exhaust himself – in a sequence that became famous as 'Rope a Dope'. If you see the sequence again, look at Ali's eyes. Despite the pounding, not once does he appear to doubt himself, not once does he lose faith, not once does he believe in anything but his own ultimate victory. There are echoes of this with Steve Case in the mid-nineties. I am exhausted from just listing the blows he and AOL took, and I've missed a good few out.

I'll pick a big one to finish this sequence. Later in the decade, after a variety of lawsuits (including some class actions) pursuing a variety of causes, the whole future of ISPs in general, and AOL in particular, was put on the line by the threat of the Communications Decency Act (CDA) that lumbered through the US courts in the mid 1990s.

There is, of course, a ton of good news about the Internet. The bad news is that nobody has really thought through the full implications of the medium regarding, for instance, bomb makers and sexual predators. The CDA proposed onerous restrictions and penalties on the ISPs if they 'allowed' unsuitable sexual material anywhere on their sites or in their chat rooms. It was, of course, a manifestation of the anally retentive conservative backlash that mobilises quite regularly in the US, and its analysis and proposals were preposterous bollocks. But it took a long time, and a journey to the US Supreme

Court, and the dedication and determination of AOL's in-house at-torneys, for it to be so deemed.

Enough. The US Supreme Court ruled on the CDA in 1997, and another dragon was slain. I haven't just made the point – I think I've hammered it, despite my attempts at brevity. There may be more to this Dream, but one part of it is surely, The Dream Borne By Beating Continuous Adversity.

Let me pause for a breath. You go and get a cuppa, or a glass of something with a bit more sting in it, because there *is* more to this Dream and this Dream Merchant.

I stayed with AOL through all of the above. Increasingly, I had new alternatives as well as CompuServe, Prodigy and MSN. I got pissed off with the AOL engaged signal, and being cut off far too quickly after I had switched to unlimited use pricing. Yet, in the age of the virtually unsatisfiable consumer, I stayed with AOL, along with millions of others. Eventually the Churners came back too. Eventually the investors also returned to the fold – in 1998 AOL's stock price grew 600%. Way to go, Steve.

There was something about this brand that captured the *zeitgeist* of the nineties. We were all going three steps back and then four paces forward. Apart from an elite of techno-geeks, a big part of two genera-tions of people were keen to become enfranchised users of new tech-nology, and both (albeit to a different degree) needed help to get there. There is no doubt that DOS and then Windows (with all due respect to Apple) opened the doors to PC usage for these people. Equally, there can be no doubt that AOL opened the door to cyberspace. It was quite clear to me from the moment I heard the famous verbal 'Welcome' word from the Voice of AOL when I logged on – followed a wee bit later by 'You've got mail' and 'File's done'. I was among friends.

I was under no illusion that the technology involved in all this was way beyond my ken (which is still the case – and maybe more so), but somebody was putting this massively complex technology to use in a way that *made it easy for me*. I could e-mail peers. I could book and buy stuff on the Web. And, yes, I could be seen to be doing these things.[6] It also provided what I wanted, in a way I wanted it. CompuServe and Prodigy were driven by supply-side goals, but Steve Case saw in his strategy of the three 'C's – communications, community and clarity – exactly what the demand side wanted. Even if it couldn't quite articulate it for itself.

Icons were used for ease of operation. The 'keyword' concept was introduced to dumb-down the technology even further. Installation was easy. After the first battle with Microsoft, the first uneasy peace between the two adversaries saw AOL's icon appear on Windows desktops, and AOL accepting Internet Explorer as its default browser. With hindsight, it seems that AOL won the peace as well.

In 1994 Steve Case hired Barry Schuler to design AOL's screens, and liked the results so much he bought his company (and him) one year later. Now CEO of AOL, Shuler's philosophy is simple but profound: *'Normal people don't lust after technology. They want whatever it's supposed to do'.*[7] This is the man who Case entrusted with what I see and do when I log in to AOL. This Dream might be an example of surviving adversity, but it is also a wondrous example of a *Dream Borne Of Using the Most Complex Technology to Make Life Simple For The Customer*.

There is one more dimension to this man. By any conventional measure, he has been hugely successful but, at first glance, it would seem to be a fair conclusion that his achievements came *in spite of* his personality, *in spite of* his way of doing things and *in spite of* his general character. He still appears boyish and introvert – very un-chairman-like and un-CEO-ish. He is close to only a few people, and remains distant from most. During an in-company analysis, he was identified as introverted, intuitive, thinking and perceptual. He has been described as placid and quietly observant.

All the above does not sound promising HowBoy material. But if you push the spade down a foot or so deeper, and turn some more

---

[6] This is important, but is largely a male thing. It is estimated that 90% of what males do or buy is for the effect it might have on others.
[7] Quoted in *Business Week*, June 2001.

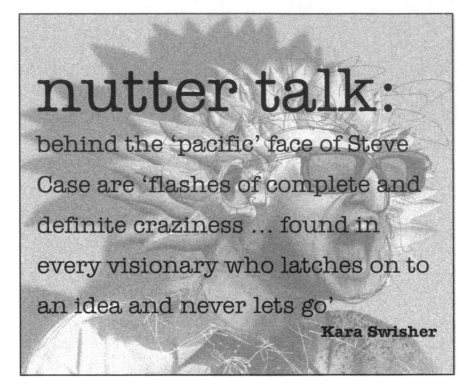

nutter talk:

behind the 'pacific' face of Steve Case are 'flashes of complete and definite craziness ... found in every visionary who latches on to an idea and never lets go'

Kara Swisher

stuff over, a new picture emerges. If you are stranded in a corporate foxhole under enemy fire, this is a man you want in there with you. Yeah, he's quiet and observant, but he soaks stuff in like a sponge. Then, when a decision is needed, he'll take it – solo if required, and as fast as needs be – and it will be worth waiting for. He never seems to lose sight of the required direction of the business, whatever the deflection. And they surely had enough of those. He is bloody-minded, persistent and resilient – how else could he have soaked up all those blows?

Is he a tad Machievellian? Is he ever. He's been called a liar, sleazy, a soap salesman and a fool. Behind the 'pacific' face of the guy there are 'flashes of complete and definite craziness ... found in every visionary who latches on to an idea and never lets go'.[8] In my

---

[8] Quoted: *AOL.com*, Kara Swisher (Times Books, 1998).

judgement he evidenced all these sins – and more – on assorted occasions during the white-water ride of the 1990s. Mostly, he did what he had to do to hang on to a Dream. Those of us who never delivered a Dream should pause, reflect – and maybe learn a thing or two.

The Dream was built on the two great strengths we have covered, and it was built by a great Dream Merchant. No commentary should underestimate, however, the contribution made by the spirit, skill and behaviour of the man himself. Without this HowBoy, the Dream might not have made it through till the dawn.

NUTTER SCORE:

Dream Merchant: Four stars

HowBoy: Four stars

JÜRGEN SCHREMPP

7

WE HEAD TO EUROPE FOR OUR NEXT CANDIDATE, which is more than a tad embarrassing for some of us. The reason being that I could subtitle this section as: 'Is it possible that a Tosser can be a Dream Merchant or a HowBoy?[1]

In this section I want to explore the idea that a real nasty bastard can build a dream and/or a record of great achievement that compares with those who have done that via more positive routes.

I spent a lot of time picking one out of a short list. I wanted a real gem – the kind you would write an unauthorised biography about and call it *A True Shit*. In truth, I wanted to use Al 'Chainsaw' Dunlap

---

[1] Bearing in mind my potential American audience, I need to translate this. For 'Tosser' my American readers should substitute the word 'Asshole'.

– he of the tyrannical pursuit of shareholder value, who finally destroyed it and himself in a Sunbeam in the US. I only abandoned him when even I realised that a guy who has disappeared from sight, with any dream he had neatly around his ankles, wouldn't do my deranged thesis much good.

I ended up picking a German, and – before anybody yells or gets insulted – let me plead guilty to some racial stereotyping. Don't get me wrong here. The Germans are a fine bunch of folk, with many skills, and I love my BMW – but they really have no idea why the rest of the world dislikes them so much. We, in the rest of the world, are, of course, crystal clear on the subject.[2]

I can't help it. Run with me here for a minute or two. Imagine you were casting for a future James Bond movie. Some groovy hunk has been cast as JB, and a suitably gorgeous female co-star has signed to play his love interest. Now, all you need is a villainous stereotype to threaten the world, and the job's a good 'un. Now, let's see. How about a ruthless, power hungry, bespectacled, chain-smoking Aryan male? He speaks English with a German accent. He has a history of exploiting people, and in some cases peoples. He has a behavioural track record in the apartheid era in South Africa that doesn't bear over-analysis – one of his earlier 'successes' was supplying 'W' class luxury cars to the white elite in that tortured country. Most of those cars doubled as potential military vehicles. He is driven by winning, is intolerant of weakness, occasionally tormented and thrives on physical danger. His vision is selective (at best) and one-eyed (at worst).

In all honesty, if you came up with that profile you'd be laughed out of the initial script reading. It's just too stereotyped and over the top. Somebody might file it for a future Austin Powers spoof.

It is, however, a summary description of the man who has been described as one of the most powerful global (business) leaders of

---

[2] In my case it is because, with two NOTABLE exceptions, they have spent my life beating us at soccer. Others have their own reasons.

the new millennium, and personally engineered the world's largest industrial merger with the formation of DaimlerChrysler AG. The sheer size of that achievement, and his role in making it happen, qualify him for consideration as a Dream Merchant. The impact of his style – such as it is – necessitates that we consider him as a How-Boy. Are there things we can learn that we can use in our personal game plans?

If you do any research on this guy, you will have to digest many adjectives – at least from those people who are prepared to be quoted.[3] Some descriptive words, like 'ruthless' and 'nasty', crop up again and again. It is true, however, that, among these many negative words, there are some that are positive – such as 'compelling' and 'winning'.

To get to the heart of this, we need to get behind some of these words. In 1989 when I flew to Miami to take up my job with Burger King, my reading on the plane consisted of a six-inch-thick wad of press cuttings on the company. Virtually all of them, when writing about BK, contained the same negative keywords – poor service, scruffy and tired. I found them frustrating and useless – they didn't tell me how, when, why or where our service let us down, or our system appeared tired, or we looked scruffy. They were just tired epithets that journalists and commentators typed in on autopilot when they wrote about Burger King. Without more information, you can't understand what a 'tired' system is, and if you don't understand it, you can't fix it.

If this guy's Dream and *modus operandi* were built on being ruthless and nasty, we need to know more about the how, when, why and where. Then we can understand and make judgements. Then we can decide if any or all of them can work for us. In short – we need to develop a Tosser's Charter. Using Schrempp's track record, I'm going to outline a bunch of elements I see in his make-up and

---

[3] There are many who won't comment openly – genuinely fearing potential consequences.

approach. Together they make up a formula for achieving a Dream his way. When that's done, we can reflect and make judgements.

Let me start with the easy one. It's about a love of winning. I'll now follow that by opening my own kimono – I quite like winning as well. If the truth were known, whether it was in my less-than-celebrated amateur soccer days, or a game of golf, or a head-to-head in a business market or shortlist for a job, I was pissed off if I lost. I still am. One of my greatest frustrations at politicians (who normally don't bother me too much because I pay them no attention) was in the 1970s, when the UK's nanny-state, anti-Darwinism (old) Labour party tried to remove all aspects of competition from the nation's schoolrooms and school playing fields. All they proved is that you can remove the structure and facilities, but that you can't kill the spirit. It is basic human nature.

Let me add another uncomfortable truth – that most of us like winning. If you show me somebody who insists that they are relaxed about constantly losing out, I will show you somebody who lies – inwardly and/or outwardly. The occasional celebration of what Tom Peters calls 'small victories' is the staff of life to most of us, it's like an apple a day keeping the doctor away.

There is a difference, however, between the joys of winning that most of us feel, and the emotional drive that energises these tyrants. For them winning is not enough – there has to be a loser, and their kicks come mostly from looking over the net at the vanquished party. *Winning is about celebrating victory AND someone else's defeat.*

There is a big difference, and it is important in business and for the outcome of this weird thesis. One of the modern equivalents of a fable by Aesop has it that if you get two Big Cheeses[4] from modern western capitalism in a bar in the early evening and stoke 'em up with a few cocktails, you have the basis of a long night's entertainment on your hands. What you do is draw a line on the floor between

---

[4] It is best if you use the standard stereotype – a white male, aged somewhere about the mid-fifties.

them, and tell them the rules – that the winner is the one who convinces the other to come over his side of the line. The results are often hilarious, and can last through until dawn. One thing these guys have to do in these circumstances is to win. Sorry, *two* things these guys have to do in these circumstances – the other is not to lose.

Now, so rumour has it, if you do the same thing in China or Japan, it will all be over in minutes. One guy will say to the other: 'I'll come over to your side if you'll come over to mine, simultaneously'. They are back at the bar, smiling, before you've taken your seat. For them, it is important that there is no winner and loser. That nobody gains face at another's expense. It is important that both parties emerge as 'lesser winners', and that an agreement has both parties smiling. Now, pause and think: if that were a business deal, which would be the more *sustainable* solution?[5]

Schrempp evidences this need to conquer, and be seen to conquer, at every turn. In his early days, tennis was his hobby. The game, the companionship and the competition were never enough, he had to dominate and destroy his opponent. You can then join the dots right through to his finest hour – the 'merge' of Daimler and Chrysler. Right at the vinegar stroke, with all the due diligence done and the complex architecture of the deal agreed, Schrempp *threatened to pull out* unless Daimler was listed first in the new company name. He had to win. Robert Eaton, his counterpart in Chrysler, had to be seen to lose.

I struggled to articulate this next element in the psychological make-up of these guys, but it has a militaristic dimension. I ended up like John Cleese in the immortal 'Don't mention the war' episode of Fawlty Towers – in trying to avoid stating the obvious, all you do is emphasise it by other means. It is as though, given the inconvenience of the absence of a handy battlefield (which, let's be honest, is not

---

[5] Apparently, the 'eastern' approach is more likely to be the one adapted by women in the west. Which MAY explain why they don't make enough of the top positions. It may also explain why, when they do, that they generally make a better job of it than their male counterparts.

nutter talk:

'Mr Schrempp's management was not holy, not holy'

**Goodman Jordan
SAAWU unionist**

normally a handicap for a German male), they bring that approach and mentality into their business lives. *They become Warlords.*

Part of this is a physical thing. It is about 'leading' by being stronger. It is about thriving on physical danger. It is definitely *macho.* In Schrempp's case, his hard-drinking, long-hours, little-sleep, physically-in-your-face reputation is embellished by his early days playing trumpet while a coterie of old Luftwaffe fighter pilots met at his first Mercedes branch and sang their songs of, er, whimsical nostalgia. He is never happier than when taking serious personal risks hanging off a cliff face. On a family holiday in South Africa, he was responsible for a road crash that left him badly lacerated. The stitches then inhibited him from playing a full part in the camping holiday that he insisted went ahead. So, he slugged a load of brandy and took them out – all 36 of them – on his own, and carried on with open wounds. Much to his family's delight I'm sure. A regular John Wayne is our Jürgen.

These guys do have relationships, *but they are strictly two-dimensional*. Everybody else in the world is in one of two camps to these guys – either for them, or against them. One source,[6] with years of first-hand experience of Schrempp-watching, but who still will not give his name, states it bluntly:

> *'If you choose to support him, he will defend you beyond the bounds of reasonableness ... but if you oppose him, be careful ... he will demolish you'*

Schrempp was not the first, nor will he be the last Big Cheese to leave his wife and take up with another woman. In his case, however, it seems far from the normal pattern – of trading in an old one for a new 'trophy' model. What seems to have broken the old relationship and forged the new one is all to do with support. His wife of many years – long-supporting and long-suffering – stopped supporting his manic and all encompassing drive for power and conquest. So he turned to someone who 'understood' his personal odyssey and who would give him the support he craved – his personal assistant. Incidentally, this relationship, which still exists today, evolved much to the angst of the PCP (Politically Correct Police) in the US side of DaimlerChrysler, so some good came of it.

On to the next arrow in the quiver of these beasties. They are quite capable of *killing and eating their friends* if they form any sort of barrier to an immediate goal. Jürgen's path is littered with the bleached bones of people who were once his friends and allies, and one stands out in particular. Edzard Reider was chairman of the old Daimler-Benz in the early 1990s. His approach to management and leadership differed in many ways from Schrempp's, who was much

---

[6] Quoted in Jürgen Grässlin's biography: *Jürgen Schrempp – and the making of an Auto Dynasty* (McGraw Hill 1998).

more of a hands-on control freak. This had not stopped the two of them developing a close relationship, which had been profoundly influential in the latter's meteoric rise through to the periphery of power in the company. Reider was a mentor, supporter and friend. He was Schrempp's senior by sixteen years, and by all accounts treated him as a corporate son.

Schrempp demolished him. He just took him off at the knees. How he out-politicked and out-manoeuvred the elder man to take his position and then discard him like a used Kleenex is long and complex and does not belong here. That he had the stomach to do it and then face himself in the shaving mirror the next morning does belong here. The fact that he could then block out all his rear-view mirrors and get on with life as though nothing untoward had happened also belongs here. Together they illustrate the nature of this particular beast. *Et tu, Brute?* All justified in the name of shareholder value (see later).

These guys also give the impression they are *tormented.* They seem to wrestle constantly with inner demons. I am not qualified to parade anybody else's psyche in public, and I'm WAY out of my technical depth here – hence my view they give the impression of torment. It is my belief, however, that any detached observation of Schrempp would indicate that if you opened him up you would not find a Sea of Tranquillity. He can't sit still. He doesn't walk, he struts. One activity must follow the previous one without a gap, and preferably with an overlap. Work hours are long, sleep hours are short. His pace is relentless and frenetic. He chain smokes, carrying a spare pack of Marlboro just in case he gets caught short somewhere. His fuse length, in dealing with people, including those inside his inner circle, is so small it is invisible to the naked eye.

Now then. There is a difference between being restless and being tormented. I know, because I was frequently described as the former, and I took it as a compliment. If it was true I found it to be a big help. Restlessness in business, however, is born of enthusiasm and energy, mixed up with curiosity and some frustration. It doesn't devour you, or the people around you. It is also compatible with being a lazy bugger at times (and I should know). It also allows you to smell some roses on the way. There is no inner peace with Schrempp, and he was raised on an entirely different Jesus. He rants, therefore he is.

Now for the meaty stuff. These people are intolerant of weakness. The highlight reel of Schrempp's life in business illustrates this time and again, with one example that fascinates me particularly. As far back as 1957, way before Schrempp's time, after an ugly strike, Mercedes workers won the right to full sick-leave pay. For some reason, four decades later, Schrempp took them (aka the unions) on again on this very subject – leading, and being seen to lead, a combine of the biggest German automakers in an attempt to reduce sick pay. This is all the more bizarre because it was against a background of an already massively 'successful' reduction of the Daimler-Benz workforce[7] in the 1990s, which had been achieved by and large without damaging industrial action.

Why this particular issue? Why this particular battlefield? Schrempp could, and did, defend his position by trotting out quotes from what sounds like a bad German translation of Adam Smith ('We could not charge a higher price for our cars in the showrooms just because we put a sticker on them saying *constructed with full sick leave pay*'), but I go back to my question: why this particular issue? He lost this battle with the union and lost a lot of car sales. He suffered an embarrassing set back to his rapidly expanding Midas reputation. My belief is that the principle of full sick leave just sticks in his craw. It is made even more bizarre, and highlights some of the complexities of this man, by the fact that he took this on in parallel with leading the fight to *establish* other basic worker rights. I can only deduce that his approach to the 'weakness' of being sick is that it's somebody else's problem – either the person who is sick, or their

---

[7] Between 1991 and 1996 the board of Daimler reduced the workforce by nearly 90,000 employees.

family, or the state. Sickness must not be allowed to get in the way of the business at hand.

This one doesn't go away. Amazingly, he didn't take the hint. In 1998, he took on the unions again, as part of the post-merger rationalisation of DaimlerChrysler. And he took 'em on head-to-head on the same issue with a programme clearly aimed at reducing both blue-collar and white-collar sick leave. With documented and measurable success criteria identified, he switched from the stick to the carrot. A tiered bonus system was introduced, which *rewarded* you if you *weren't* sick and/or weak. Published bulletins and charts recording workers comparative absenteeism accompany the programme.

Schrempp clearly cannot tolerate weakness in himself, and this, I suppose, can be classed as a strength. That he cannot tolerate it in others does not strike me as a model for enlightened capitalism or an energised and motivated workforce. Indeed, these may prove to be *the* two essential ingredients for a sustainable modern business dream.

I've saved the big one for last. I'll leave the choice to you: this is about these guys being *exploitative*, or *one-eyed users of others*. In Schrempp's case, it is easy: in my view, he's both. Whether it is with an individual, or whole groups of people, he has a history of taking just what he needs out of a situation, and ignoring any collateral damage.

There is no doubt, for example, that Schrempp's achievements during his time with Daimler in South Africa were critical to his subsequent success. Without his success there, he would not have been in a position to make the moves he made to oust Reider and win the chairmanship. What cannot also be in any doubt was that you would have had to be deaf, dumb and blind not to have not felt the winds of change in that troubled country in the mid-1980s, when our hero was there. There is no way of fancying it up – a (relatively) rich, white minority suppressed a poor, black majority in a regime of oppression that belonged in another century. Many whites that were part of apartheid survived it, and seek to justify it as being something necessary for the time and the place. They claim it is easy to sit and pontificate from a distance, and that it wasn't like that at all, and that you had to be there to understand the complexities. What bollocks.

Jürgen's role in all this was to sell elite cars – called 'W' class just to add insult to any injury – to the white elite. Oh, and by the way, the majority of them were designed so they had a dual military purpose. His defence to the charge that he used apartheid to further his career is that the company and the world in general have analysed his role there openly, and concluded he did nothing 'wrong' – although the military 'dual-use' of the vehicles bothered him then and still does. So, that's OK then.

Whoever you are, whatever the circumstances – if you can be used and/or exploited, you *will be* by this guy. You can bank on it. The 89,000 job losses in Daimler in the early 1990s (which are still rising, by the way) don't anger me so much – he wasn't the only one to inherit a bloated organisation at a time when technology was offering huge productivity gains. That's the nature of change, and the price we in society pay for progress and living in a wonderful world. What I'm talking about is different – Schrempp's calculated use of people as a means to his end. If the circumstances are vaguely amoral, or it involves a bit of oppression, hey – *c'est la guerre* baby.

Right. We have a formula for building a Dream based on tyranny. We have a formula for the achievement of glory via the route of being a HowBoy-shit. You need a heaped teaspoonful of each of the following:

- celebrate your victories *and* the defeat of your opponents;
- become a Warlord;
- have only two-dimensional relationships. People are with you or not. There is no other position;
- kill and eat your friends if need be;
- evidence torment and inner demons;
- don't tolerate weakness (in yourself or others);
- exploit and use others. Ignore collateral damage; and
- use only one eye if it helps your cause.

That is a list consisting of eight dimensions. There is a ninth, and it is the one that throws this whole analysis into chaos. *These guys can score runs, and lots of them.* Following that formula, Schrempp delivered an almighty Dream – the biggest industrial merger in history.

I have concentrated, deliberately, on the negatives of this man and his ride to fame. Now, consider this: in 1997 alone, 715,000 Mercedes were sold, more than 11% higher than the previous year. Against a background of thousands of 'old' jobs lost, jobs that had really ceased to exist, the company created 12,000 new ones. 80% of those car sales were in products less than five yeas old. Operating profits were up by 79%, and *all these figures relate to the last period prior to the merge with Chrysler.*

Just prior to the mega-deal, Schrempp outlined a crazy forecast – that the company's sales would be more than doubled by 2008. He achieved that figure, via the merger, within a year.

There can be no question. Measure it how you will, this is Big League success. Schrempp is not to many people's taste, including mine – but some of that can be put down to the fact that we haven't the wherewithal to behave the way he did. Although he takes it to extremes, most of us could use a bit more of some of these 'talents' in our own make-up, and frankly we would be more effective and efficient for it. Elements of his behaviour are simply Machiavellian, and are present to some degree in a good schoolteacher who needs to keep control of a class and educate reluctant pupils. Schrempp's pattern of extreme behaviour was added to by many positive talents. They are talents of which we can all be jealous – high energy, confidence, initiative, determination, always well prepared and with an analytical mind.

If we look at his results, and mix in the man's clear strengths, can we balance the whole thing and justify this man as a Dream Merchant or a HowBoy that we can respect? Should we use him as a role model for our journeys?

Answer: NO.

Let me press the fast forward button – and hold my finger on it right through until April 11 in the year 2001. The place is Berlin, the occasion is the shareholders meeting of DaimlerChrysler AG. In the three or four years the tape moved forward, there has been a dramatic change in the climate. Our hero is a now a villain. Shareholders are calling for his head. One holds up a clock, telling Schrempp it is time for him to go. Another stockholder, my favourite because of his name – Lars Labryga[8] – stands up and accuses Schrempp of the unthinkable – that he *has halved shareholder value*. Lars is right – in the blinkered approach to the Holy Grail hunt for shareholder value, he has destroyed it. As I write, the market value of DaimlerChrysler is less than that of Daimler-Benz alone before the merger.

The Dream is in a mess all right – and my belief is that the problems arise from the nature of the way it was built. The deep issues are with Chrysler, and the later acquisition of 34% of Mitsubishi. These were not synergistic acquisitions. They are like a mongoose and two cobras stapled together inside one of those plastic supermarket bags. They were acquired because they could be. They were acquired for the love of conquest and the pursuit of power.

Time and again history has shown us, if a dream is built on these foundations, it is not sustainable. If you need a proving example, just read the history of the Balkans over the last millennium. You can hold it when times are good, but when pressure is applied, cracks appear. Things burst out of chests like they did in the *Alien* movie. There is nothing *to build on*.

Schrempp's response to this crisis has been typically smash-mouth. Output is cut, and another 25,000 collateral-damage jobs are doomed. Yawn. In a 'Fuck-you' approach to his suppliers, they were mandated to reduce costs by a named percentage. So much for partnerships. Snore. Downstream, car distributors and dealers, many with their total life's equity in the balance sheet of their businesses,

---

[8] His name spells Raray Balls if you play around with it long enough. It doesn't take much to amuse me.

have been given abrupt notice of termination. Er … so much for partnerships again. Groan, fart.

The future of DaimlerChrysler is a crapshoot. Global engineering, and vast untapped economies of scale by forcing *genuine* common-part synergies on the three automobile companies might work, along with all the slash and burn stuff. It won't matter for Schrempp. For him, the war is over.

I have a pile of notes on the guy, and it would take me thirty seconds to find out how old he is, but I can't be bothered. Besides, I'm not sure what it would translate to in our earth years. It doesn't matter. Whatever it is, my belief is that within half a decade he'll be moving in next door to Al 'Chainsaw' Dunlap in a home for retired schoolyard bullies somewhere in Florida. He's in the process of being found out. His Dream was a dinosaur. It was Big, but it was one of those where being Big was no help. In fact, quite the opposite. It ended up having to stand in water to stay upright. His Dream had no staying power, and his Neanderthal way of achieving it was a big part of the problem.

NUTTER SCORE:

Dream Merchant: One star (see me)

HowBoy: One star

RICHARD BRANSON

8

I T'S TOUGH TO BE OBJECTIVE about this guy. Everybody has a point of view. Apparently, more than 90% of UK consumers recognise the brand name Virgin, and – incredibly – the same percentage recognise Branson's name in association with it. I suspect that a sub-analysis would indicate that these people either love or hate him.

Objectivity is even harder if you have met him. I'm not sure 'met' works as a definition to cover the fleeting occasion where our ships passed within hailing distance. I am sure he won't remember it. It was enough for me to ensure I remember him as a PLT.[1]

The occasion was some fancy institutional business lunch within the Square Mile – London's historic financial district. I think it was

---

[1] Pompous Loud Tosser.

the Guildhall. It was full of British industry's Finest, and I scrambled in off the subs bench for GrandMet – as a stand-in for somebody who cleverly invented an excuse to be somewhere else. I was placed at a table opposite Branson; offset about two places to his left. He was late, and arrived wearing a scruffy woollen sweater. The clothing contrast was stark. We were all suitably dressed for a City luncheon and, apart from mine, there wasn't a suit at our table that cost less than a thousand pounds. He took his place without comment or apology.

The lunch was partly sponsored by British Airways. This sponsorship involved them coughing up a few grand, and bought them the right to have their corporate name on the menu – which they folded into a six-inch model of one of their planes. This is well before the Dirty Tricks[2] campaign hit the headlines, but it would be safe to say that, had both companies been in bed together, neither would have climbed over Jennifer Lopez to go and make love to the other one. Branson's reaction when he saw the little model of his rival airline's flagship, sitting in front of him, was instant. Without a word, he picked his up and threw it, with the menu, under the table.

My, how we laughed.

Anyway, once we have got over the fact that occasionally, when he appears on TV, my wife has to lock her knicker drawer to stop me getting at the Luger, we need to figure him out.

How is it that a pompous, eternal fifth-former justifies himself in this elite company of Dream Merchants and HowBoys? Because that is exactly what he does. At the highest level of both.

Almost single-handedly, he has reinvented the science of branding. In the process he has created, arguably,[3] Britain's first global

---

[2] In 1993, Virgin won a £610,000 legal remedy against BA as a result of a long campaign by the latter to inflict assorted trading damages on the former. Relations between the two companies were acrimonious to say the least.

[3] This is fun to argue after a few drinks. The fact that my buddies in Diageo argue the case for Baileys Irish Cream, in my observation, kinda emphasises Branson's claim rather than damages it.

brand for fifty years – an appalling indictment of my country with its commercial and global heritage. In addition, the changes in branding that have come about because of him, or around him, or in spite of him (delete as you wish) are irrevocable. Whatever role he played in the transition (and I believe it to be seminal), when he started out branding was about *what* a company did (largely defined by its portfolio of product or services). Thirty years after he started his mail-order record business – famously, and in his words, from a telephone booth and with less capital than most couples would spend on a meal in a restaurant – the science of branding has become much more about *how* a company delivers its products or services to its market.

For a hundred years, branding was about products. Hoover, Coca-Cola, Heinz, Rolls Royce (and many more) became mighty organisations built around branded products. Distinction – that wonderful one-word definition of the goal of effective and efficient branding – was all about the product, its price, its specification, its 'new improved formula' and its mass marketing to its masses of existing and potential customers.

The Virgin brand, however, is not about the price or specification of any one of its more than one hundred and fifty products and services. It is about creating a business personality, which signals quite specific values and attributes that attract a broad base of consumers. The consumers will then try the individual products and services, and that's when you micro-market to them to increase loyalty, raise purchase frequency and jack up average spend.

The results of this changing science are profound – particularly in the case of some of the dinosaurs. McDonalds – known for fifty years for a limited range of products and a one-dimensional corporate persona – suddenly took leave of their senses and acquired a branded, espresso-coffee retailer. Without pausing for breath, they followed that by investing in Mexican food brands, rotisserie chicken operations and opened a hotel in Switzerland targeted at *the*

business traveller.[4] Coca-Cola recently sent Doug Ivester, the personally groomed successor to the legendary Roberto Goizuetta, for an
early shower after just a few months in the job. From all accounts,
what he was doing wasn't the problem; it was *how* he was relating
to the Coca-Cola's massive stakeholder base and the outside world.
They then pondered awhile behind closed doors – and emerged
having chosen somebody called Douglas Daft to succeed him. Disney couldn't beat that. I rest my case.

In figuring out how Branson shaped and delivered this Dream,
we run into trouble. There is no evidence that this was a planned
journey. In fact, the opposite seems the case. It is doubtful that you
could find a less likely candidate to mastermind a worldwide business epiphany. He had no business school heritage, in fact virtually
no higher education at all. Photographs from the early seventies
show a scruffy hippie – which is rather embarrassing to me, as I believe I had a pair of bell bottomed trousers that more than matched
anything he had. There is no evidence of a James Dyson-style jigsaw
coming together. There is no evidence of early life influences linking up with a prepared intellect, and that mix, in turn, slotting together with a specific technical challenge – and then all that coming
together in a blinding business breakthrough. On the other hand,
his approach is too structured, and the results have been so consistently effective, for it all to be put down to happenstance. This is no
goofball being dragged unwittingly from success to success. There is
some science, there is much intuition, some things are subconscious
and there is some fortune.

Branson has one attribute that we haven't come across before
in this book. It is present, however, albeit in smaller quantities and in

---

[4] I find this unbelievable – although I heap praise on them for the other stuff.
They need to know what they are up against. I am the stereotypical business
traveller, and if I was visiting Switzerland, and there were NO OTHER ROOMS
AVAILABLE IN THE WHOLE COUNTRY, I still would not stay at a McDonalds
hotel. If they removed my trousers and threatened to play the blue bit of the flame
from a butane torch on my 'nads unless I checked in, I would still refuse. Good
luck to them.

different manifestations, in other Dream Merchants *and* HowBoys. This guy is a walking bundle of conflicts. As a result, he is almost completely unpredictable, and more than a little mysterious. This applies to him and his businesses. The seamless combination of both has been likened to somebody playing out on the street, but whose house keeps the curtains drawn.

This built-in conflict thing fascinates me – only because I am convinced it has played a big part in his success. Consider the following claims I make about him:

- *He is a Professional Amateur*. Time and again we see evidence of a surface buffoon who seems to have missed out on basic business professionalism. He failed elementary maths at school, and makes a big deal of it. Then, on the next page, we read of his relentless and ruthless negotiating skills, his uncanny memory for detail, his nose for an opportunity and his frequent and infuriating renegotiation of 'done-deal' contracts. He is also known for his reliance on a kitchen cabinet of expert advisors.
- *He is Ruthlessly Affable*. We see lots of evidence of an easy-going, fun-to-work-with (and for), life-and-soul-of-the-party animal. He is on first names terms with his employees. He travels with, and stays in the same hotels as, his flight crews. Then, on the next page of the Book of Branson, we see pictures of the bleached bones of people that have crossed him, or lost their usefulness.
- *He is a Controlling Empowerer*. Working for Branson is fun. Work is an adventure, with hard play linked with hard work. Accountability and responsibility is devolved to good people. Businesses are autonomous. The surface picture can appear as a vaguely linked network of loosely related businesses under the common brand sign, with Branson spitting out an idea a week and a bunch of guys going off and chasing another dream. Maybe they'd report back on success or failure after a couple of years.

This surface picture is almost total bollocks. Behind the drawn curtains of Virgin another scenario exists. This alternate picture is

of highly pressurised employees, not well paid unless they create wealth through owning equity in their own bit of Virgin (i.e.
not the total group), with the parts *and* the sum of the parts of the
empire rigidly controlled by a kitchen cabinet of highly-powered
executives aided by a gaggle of central accountants, lawyers and
banks.

- *He is a Strategic Guerrilla.* If you listen to his spoutings, you hear
a visionary. You hear descriptions of broad-brush shapes, of missions and macro-level strategy. If you close your ears and watch,
however, you see a company seemingly centred on a mosaic of
his high profile tactics, his eye for detail and his control-freak nature.

These built-in conflicts, most of which are fertilised and developed
deliberately by Branson, have been critical in getting the man and
the brand to where they are today. They enable him to run the
world's first multinational street-corner kiosk. The conflicts work on
a number of levels. They enable him to be whatever his audience
wants him to be – and that audience may be made up of customers,
business partners, employees, the general public or politicians. Or
all of the above, or many others. These conflicts also enable him to be
a chameleon – adaptable to any circumstances, location or climate.

You could play around and apply many more seemingly tauto-
logical descriptions of him – and it is this built-in conflict that mud-
dies up our analysis of him as a Dream Merchant or HowBoy.

Most of the other names in this *magnum opus* are predominantly
one or the other. Some are both. Branson confuses us because he is
not one or the other, and neither is he both. Somehow, he blends the
two concepts into one.

The demented Scottish comedian, Billy Connolly, buried somewhere on a treasured cassette I have of his, does a lovely piss-take
of a bog-standard vicar trying to excite his flock during the weekly
sermon. With a crystal clear voice, not lacking in decibels, said vicar
delivers the line: *'I am one in Him, and He is one in me'.* If you've at-

tended a church service and stayed awake through the sermon, you know exactly the tone. It is delivered in a manner that enables it to be heard in the village pub three blocks away, and which prohibits it from being anything other than a statement of the blindingly obvious. Of course you understand it, it's pretty obvious innit? It's just that, if you actually stop and think about it, it is entirely unhelpful to the immediate problem of your Uncle Harry getting cancer of the colon, and you lose the plot.

If it doesn't help us solve the meaning of life, however, it does help us with Branson. His Dream Merchant *is* the HowBoy. He is one in it, and it is one in him. No matter how much he pontificates after the event about how he deliberately shaped Virgin as a *keiretsu*, it is *how* he thought and behaved (i.e. his *modus operandi*) that actually became the Dream Shape. Business schools now spend thousands of hours analysing Virgin, and business gurus squeak on endlessly on the same subject. In my observation, and to quote the immortal

nutter talk:

'I believe there is almost no limit to what a brand can do, but only if used properly'

Richard Branson

words of the *Spinal Tap* member looking at Elvis' grave: *'You can have too much fucking perspective'*.

Virgin's (and Branson's) alchemy is just a mix of three ingredients, i.e.:

- *Take one teaspoon of he didn't know what the hell he was doing.* Back in about 1972, as a bright young thing, I had just moved down to Shell's UK headquarters in London. I was a high flyer, and my boss – a wizened old Scot – appraised me regularly and rigorously. At our first such session, he confused me by telling me he was only going to appraise three-quarters of me. Eh? What? His logic was intriguing. He told me that there was a quarter of me that was impenetrable. It ruled itself. It did a lot of very good things and occasionally some crazy, self-destruct-type crap – but you didn't get the first bit without taking the risk of the second. It was a dark area. We should leave it alone, let it run free and manage what came out.

  I admit to being a bit confused at the time so I headed off to Gordon's Wine Bar on the Embankment and got gently bladdered, and haven't really thought about it much since. But, without paralleling myself in any way with Branson, that analysis applies to him. There's a bit of him that is dark and odd, and he trusts it. He doesn't know what he will do before the event, and he doesn't know why he did it after. When you look at the total, a lot more good things happen than bad.
- *Add another teaspoon of simple, clear, commonsense rules and formulae.* There is more than enough consistency, and there are more than enough repeat patterns for it not to be all down to winging it or intuition. He has *must-dos* and *no go areas* and adheres to them rigidly.
- *Finally, add a teaspoon of the corporate and consuming world being ready for a new approach.* As we entered the Age of Aquarius, there were a lot of tired ideas about. Old branding was in its death throes (Red Barrel?). Hierarchical organisational structures were

tumbling. Investment funds were swishing about looking for winning corporate horses and jockeys. Information technology and transport logistics blew away barriers to physical trade and inhibited thinking. The old way of doing things was tired. The world was ready and waiting for the new way.

Branson's model, which resulted from mixing the ingredients together, and which then came over the hill like the Seventh Cavalry, has been documented and analysed up the Wahoo. In addition, I don't want to ignore my buddy in *Spinal Tap*. Even more important – I don't want to drift into acres of parboiled Freud and psychobabble. What is important is how many elements there are, and how they all come together in the Dream Merchant/HowBoy concoction. By my calculation there are six, so lets marshal them together and have a quick look:

1   *Branding by reputation, not product*. This mantra, fairly and correctly attributed to Branson, has been quoted so often, and now seems so obvious; it is easy to forget it was anti-Christ territory a generation ago. Nike is not about running shoes or golf balls – it is about hunting for cool things to be seen in. Branding isn't about products anymore, even 'New Improved' ones. It is about, for example, the celebration of small self-indulgences (e.g. Häagen-Dazs), or lifestyle (e.g. Starbucks). In Virgin's case, it is not about the price or specification of an airline seat, it is about an amorphous blend of 'values' such as *Fun* and *Innovation* and *Great Value*.

2   *Famous for being famous*. Branson is renown as the CEO who is a Rock Star, or at least the CEO who aspires to be one. There are a lot of new CEOs on the block who are now trying to ape him, and – let me tell you – it is tempting. About eight years ago, I had just visited the UK, and done a segment on Burger King buying Wimpy on early morning TV. Soon after, I was in a black cab, heading out to Heathrow airport, on my way back to the

US. The cabbie was looking at me in the mirror, more and more intently as we hit the outskirts of the airport. I actually thought he was struggling to put a name to a face he'd seen earlier on TV. I preened, and there is no other word for it. I gave him my good side in the rear-view mirror. Eventually, he spoke:

'Well?'

Clearly, it was not going to come to him without a clue. He needed help. I obliged.

'Er ... You may have seen me on TV this morning.'

I really heard myself saying this. I really did. I shiver to this day just thinking about it. My man responded, and flattened me with a large spade:

'No, no, no – which terminal *do you want dropping off at?'*

End of preen. It is heady and dangerous stuff this rock-star business.

The rock-star link was easy for Branson in his early years, as he allied with the likes of Mike Oldfield [*who he? Ed.*] and others of a similar kidney who were in the Virgin stable. Later it took on a different dimension. Many high-profile business leaders harbour a frustration which is that, whatever levels of wealth and business success they achieve, they have one big difference to their counterparts in entertainment and sports: *they never get asked for their autographs.*

Many of them compensate for this by buying sports franchises. In Branson's case, he simply aped the necessary behaviour of a Rock Star, and twinned in with the ageing ones as peers. Think of Branson and you think of a bad haircut, thirty years out of date, ridiculous wealth, an eroding jaw line, declining rebelliousness, staged photo-opportunities with cubic yards of cleavage and an act that, on occasion, comes dangerously close to being that of a Saddo. Dead ringer for Rod Stewart really.

3   *Master of Free Media.* One of the best business minds I know occupies the space between the ears of a guy called Richard Melman. He runs a business called Lettuce Entertain You – which

involves an eclectic network of restaurants around Chicago. Talking with him about ten years ago, I asked him about his media spend – as all his restaurants seemed to generate tremendous consumer awareness. He told me that he didn't buy media; he just bought *free* media. His marketing activity was all about generating editorial press coverage, and the seeking of that was just as expensive, and required the same levels of resource and skill, as did any conventional marketing operation.

Branson confesses to spending a third of his time in an attempt to get himself and/or Virgin in the media. He sets high targets. He is not interested in the inside pages – he wants front page positioning and headlines. If you worked out the opportunity cost of his time it equates to a multi-million media spend, which is *in addition to* the conventional spending Virgin coughs up as a brand in the normal course of events. This is a science not an art. It requires planning and execution. Branson is a master of the staged event, the photo opportunity, and the sound bite. He is also a master of the Grand Gesture – defined as one that gets prats like me writing about them in books.[5] His link with the Sex Pistols taught him the value of controlled shock tactics – and now and again he plays this card very effectively.[6] Many (most?) CEOs would have a cow at the thought of spending a third of their time on PR. To Richard, it is not an option.

4   *New-fashioned synergy.* Old-fashioned synergy was, for example, about owning a brewery and buying pubs to distribute the beer. It could be defined as the acquisition or development of

---

[5] For example – he distributed to his employees the monetary damages award from BA after the 'Dirty Tricks' lawsuit. He famously booked a couple of stranded Virgin passengers on the (British Airways) Concorde when they complained they were going to miss a family funeral. There are thousands more Branson stories like this.

[6] He launched Virgin Cola in New York with a gay marriage. Quite what one has to do with the other I don't know, *but here I am writing about it.* So it worked.

a business whose financial performance directly affected, or was affected by, other businesses within the corporate stable. Its main vehicle of activity was cross promotion or inter-group trading. Viacom buying Blockbuster Video is a prime example. Major consumer-durable selling retailers developing financial services (credit cards, insurance etc. etc.) provide another. The new-fashioned synergy is much less obvious. Under the Big Top tent of a brand's reputation and common values, a circus ring of activities goes on. These activities can seem wholly un-related. The synergy is market oriented, and market oriented by lifestyle and attitude, not product need. If the consumer is comfortable with what the brand stands for, within an ever-widening brand boundary the brand owners can keep finding services and products that will further develop the relation-ship.

5   *Assume the 'David' position.* He likes taking on giants – the big cola players, the mighty financial institutions, the huge airlines and so on. It fosters his image as a modern day consumer's Robin Hood. It also adds to the legend of the anti-establishment rebel. It also makes for canny economic sense. These giant cor-porations are often rigidly structured, slow to react to any-thing, overhead heavy, set in their ways and supply rather than demand oriented. In other words, everything he and Virgin aren't. So he can pick some low hanging fruit very quickly, and often there's enough of that for Virgin's total purposes.

6   *Wrap your mystery in an enigma.* There are similarities here to Benetton – inasmuch as you have to dig deep and long to find out what is going on inside the respective empires. For some-body with such an approachable and open personal style, what goes on behind the scenes in Virgin is as near a closed book as the law and assorted GAAP[7] charters will allow. Branson, of

---

[7] The generally agreed accounting principles that cover western commerce. Easy to dance around.

course, holds that this privacy is a Good Thing for his brand reputation – noting that if there is a short-term tail off in consumer demand for one of his products and services, he can ride it out by making a few million pounds less for a while and not bow down to short-term, external shareholder pressure to cut advertising or front-line people. It also enables him to go about his business without his failures being publicly paraded in the tabloids in financial detail – the sort of thing that has added much topspin to Marks and Spencer's turn-of-the-millennium, unshackled bungee-jump. What the tabloids don't know about, they can't parade among the nipples on Page 3. Make no mistake, this is important to Branson. He is ever the populist, and his business model suffers along with the myth if the word *failure* appears in too many mass-media sentences and sound bites.

There we are then. I was going to add one more built-in conflict to those I listed earlier. I was going to add *annoyingly likeable*. But I decided to keep it till here, because I have to score him against my criteria, and I continually swing back and forth while at the same time I blow hot and cold.[8] This is a complex man, and he causes complex reflections. The HowBoy is one within the Dream Merchant, and vice versa. All I know is this – it is easier to celebrate the positives in each of the conflicts within him than it is to whine at all the negatives. If you try the latter, after a while it sounds unmistakably like envy.

Branson reinvented branding and that's impressive enough to chisel on anybody's grave. I believe, when the history of commerce is eventually written, he will have – and deserve – a much bigger paragraph than we can conceive of today. This is despite the fact that, if he sticks his tongue out of his mouth, he looks like a haemorrhoid.

---

[8] Please do not try this at home. At least, not *after* cocktails.

I'm staying with my categories, and scoring him highly:

NUTTER SCORE:

Dream Merchant: Four stars

HowBoy: Five stars (plus a merit)

ROBERTO GOIZUETA

9

SOMETIME IN (I THINK) LATE 1991, I boarded a company-owned private Gulfstream jet at an airfield in Atlanta, Georgia.

I had access to our own company's plane, but rarely used it. For one thing, whereas I was based in Miami, the wings that were essential to my rock star/CEO kit were in a hangar up in Minneapolis, where Burger King's 'parent' company, GrandMet, was located. The other reason was that the variable cost of its use was charged out to we 'subsidiary' companies, and it was horrendous. As I was leading an internal company-austerity drive I stayed away from the (hard) cost and the (soft) negative symbolism of hauling the thing down to my headquarters so that I could fly in ludicrous luxury to my next meeting.

Being male, however, my hypocrisy was such I would never turn down a lift in one of these babies, and at the end of this particularly long and eventful day I happily settled – well, slumped really – into my leather seat on the Gulfstream.

My one travelling companion was a wee bit more fastidious. Whereas, by the end of a long day, I had usually adopted the 'crumpled' look, he was still immaculate. He took off his suit jacket, hung it on a coat hanger in the fitted closet, and donned a sort of casual 'bomber' jacket. I say 'bomber jacket', but this was not one that had been picked up off the bargain rack in Gap. It looked as though it had just been purchased from Armani, and then *ironed*. On the left breast was a rather understated brand mark. It consisted of two words, perhaps the most famous two linked words, in the most famous font style, in the history of the world: Coca-Cola.[1]

My travelling companion was Roberto Goizueta, and it was Coca-Cola's plane. I had just finished a day's business in the company's impressive headquarters in Atlanta, which culminated in a meeting with their (already) legendary CEO. The rest of my team was heading off elsewhere, but I was due back at our HQ in Miami. It so happened that Roberto was himself heading to the same location, so offered me a lift. I gladly agreed.

Our meetings had been with, at different times, Donald Keough, Roberto's straight-talking number two and sometime alterego; an effervescent marketer called Charlie Frenette and Coca-Cola's CFO, Douglas Ivester. The main work had been done, but during the journey, among many ranging subjects,[2] we recapped some of the ground we had covered and the decision we had agreed in principle. Burger King would be ditching Pepsi, and switching back to Coca-Cola. Some 7000 soda fountains were heading back to the Real Thing. I was a real popular guy in Atlanta.

---

[1] Oh, all right. Be picky. They are the *second* most famous linked words – Monica Lewinsky being in first place.

[2] I never kept diaries or notes of meetings. It frustrates me in one way that I cannot remember much of what we talked about – but that is for my own self-indulgence. If I had made notes, or could remember, they would stay with me.

In all honesty, the switch was as much about being pissed at Pepsi as being in love with Coca-Cola, and it belongs in another book for another time – but it gave me, and us, exposure to the way this company worked under a CEO who was already rewriting the record books.

From the start, Coca-Cola made it plain that they were not just in the business of supplying our 7000 restaurants with syrup concentrate. They wanted a partnership – which covered everything from technical support (and investment) to sales promotion and marketing in our outlets. They didn't want to be a supplier; they wanted to be a friend. A year or so later when our Florida headquarters was devastated by Hurricane Andrew (along with a good chunk of the south of the state), Coca-Cola were almost first on the scene with a HUGELY welcome crisis team that is on standby to respond to crises encountered by them or their customers in any corner of the globe. It is less a brand, more a way of life.

Roberto Goizueta's performance in the 16 years he was at the helm of Coca-Cola until his untimely death in 1997 is, perhaps, the exception that proves the rule that I outlined in the previous chapter on Richard Branson. The idea that brands are no longer just about single products, but about reputation and corporate personality, is now widespread and proven. Disney, for example, is now in all sorts of businesses, many not even under its own brand name. It is hard to think of a *single product* brand – a business 'one-trick pony' if you like – that has the distribution, awareness and sales equivalent of this ubiquitous drink with the closely guarded formula. In other fields, brands such as McDonalds and Microsoft, and the great automobile and consumer electronic brand names, now all have a variety of products under their brand canopies. Sure, Diet Coke is a sub brand, and there are other drinks in Coca-Cola's corporate portfolio, but if you look at the past success (and particularly Goizueta's phenomenal performance), and their future potential, the old strap line says it all: Coke Is It.

So here, we are going to analyse two things. One, the blindingly obvious – how valid is a Dream built on a one-trick pony? The second dimension will sound rather strange at this stage. I've called it The Power of a Mistake.

Goizueta took over the presidency of Coca-Cola in 1980, becoming second in command, but not yet a clear heir-apparent, to Robert Woodruff – the last of the dynasty that had, over the previous 60 years, turned a quasi-health drink into America's (and the world's) favourite manufactured non-alcoholic drink. It was twenty-six years, almost to the day, after the young Roberto had answered an advert put in a Havana newspaper by a Coca-Cola bottler in pre-Castro Cuba. Less than two years later, he was crowned king.

The story of his distressing flight from Cuba, and his corporate ascendancy, is well documented elsewhere. How this quiet, determined and capable young man could beat off a powerful peer group for the crown is also another subject – although, in passing, we should note that the graceful gentleman sitting opposite me in the Gulfstream jet that evening had, on occasion, proved himself more than capable of the required politicking and sycophancy to complement his more conventional talents.

For my analysis, the starting point ignores these. I'll kick off with the state of the Coca-Cola 'nation' at his coronation. It was not good. Pepsi was hammering it in the US.

Although Coke still had bigger overall sales, Pepsi was narrowing the gap alarmingly. It had already overtaken Coca-Cola in the crucial US supermarket sector. It was also threatening the big 'fountain' customers like McDonalds and Burger King – the latter eventually switching until the events noted at the start of this chapter.

The biggest wound of all came from the trumpeted head-to-head product 'taste' victory – espoused by Pepsi in the massively successful 'Pepsi Challenge'. To add insult to injury, the hated competition seemed to have captured the market *zeitgeist*. Michael Jackson, hugely popular and still vaguely humanoid, signed up for them, and Coca-Cola's GI-Joe imagery suddenly looked to be irrelevant for the hip, young, high-energy soft drinkers.

Sixteen years later, at the untimely end of Goizueta's tenure, Coca-Cola's market value had increased by a humble 3500%. It is a success that came largely on the back of one product, with one derivative sharing the same parent brand name. It is now Pepsi who are splashing about in the water, committing and de-committing to diversification into restaurants and snack foods.

How the hell can you take a start position of one troubled product-brand and deliver *that* Dream within one and a half decades? Just how do you get your pony to improve its one trick to that degree? That's what we need to analyse. Some of those skills might be transferable to our challenges.

Clearly it is about manic focus. I think it was Tom Peters who came up with the maxim 'If you've got more than one priority, you've got none'. Most business schools, and most business leaders preach the need for prioritisation and focus. Some live by it, some don't – but none in my experience and observation does it manically. That's because most business leaders have a choice. I don't think Goizueta believed he had any choices, *and that is his supreme wisdom.* Of course, he was helped by the fact that every time he thought he had a choice, his attempts at diversification kneed him in the groin. That should add to, not detract from, his triumphs.

I've listed six elements of this Manic Focus. While you are reading them, check them off against how you are going about building your Dream:

Prioritise *within* the priority

Even if you have just one name, like Coca-Cola, on the front of the hymnbook, there are thousands of possible hymns to sing. The everyday challenge of sourcing and using funds throws up multi-options. Every market wants to justify big budgets, but then so does the head of IT. The US bottlers don't want the brand's resources deflected into expensive, risky and long-term investments in countries whose names they can't spell. The foreign bottlers do. Should you develop new products or bolster existing ones? As Henry Ford once famously said, half your marketing budget is probably wasted – but which half?

Goizueta plotted his way through this minefield by introducing ruthless but simple Darwinism to all the projects competing for corporate resources. In later years it became known as Economic Value Added (EVA) and those three initials cover one of the most powerful elements of his heritage. Quite simply, competing internal projects were judged on the relative surpluses they generated over and above the opportunity cost of the capital (debt and/or equity) that they used.

The ruthless and consistent employment of this as an internal decision maker enabled him to justify what seemed odd decisions at the time – such as heavily gearing Coca-Cola's previously almost debt-free balance sheet to acquire substantial interests in the brand's bottlers. Later, it enabled him to justify extensive purchases of the company's own stock. These moves, all investing in that *one* brand name, brought powerful returns for investors.

Control without ownership

There is a school of management that espouses that: 'If it affects us, we must own it'. Over the years it has sent companies upstream towards primary production and supply, and downstream towards distribution and the customer interface, in the pursuit of often-misguided (and sometimes illegal) acquisitions. Another school of management preaches: 'We will own nothing but our stripped back core-competence'. This school outsources everything – almost literally in cases such as Nike. This, of course, can lead to problems at the other end of the knee-in-the-groin spectrum, as your agents, operating under your overall brand canopy, employ nine-year olds on eighty-hour weeks in third world countries.

At some stage, influence becomes control. In the case of my wife, the dividing line is a thing of beauty. It is never static, varying by circumstance and by the hour. In the case of companies, however, it usually moves from one to the other on and after the acquisition of the share that gives 51% of the entity's ownership. That kind of ownership, however, brings with it wholly different responsibilities, which are sometimes unwelcome and always deflecting.

It was Douglas Ivester, Goizueta's CFO and eventual successor, who came up with a model that could get Coca-Cola the best of both worlds – massive influence in a key area, without the unwanted deflection and responsibility of ownership. In hindsight, the '49% Solution' – i.e. the acquisition of 49% of the stock of a company whose ownership and performance was deemed key to the achievement of Coca-Cola goals – seems simple in the extreme. But it wasn't – it needed to dance through a minefield of anti-monopoly regulation almost everywhere it took place. It worked. In particular, it enabled Coca-Cola to turn an initial couple of reactive, opportunistic acquisitions of bottlers into an aggressive programme acquiring influence and *virtual* control of this crucial arm of Coca-Cola's universal market presence. In turn, the bottlers prospered on Coca-Cola's brand success, and the 49% investments generally paid back in spades for investors in the parent company. Score another point for manic focus.

Brand imperialism

This is the bit with the least relevance for most of our personal challenges, unless you sit on a mighty, mighty brand – and you are mulling your options as to the best way to global conquest. It was Warren Buffet, enticed into being a mega-investor in Coca-Cola during Goizueta's reign, who said: 'If you gave me $100 billion and said take away the soft drink leadership of Coca-Cola in the world, I'd give it back to you and say it can't be done'. Ignoring the fact that Pepsi came a bit too close for a lot less money than that in the early 1980s, by the time that decade ended Coca-Cola was the big fish in the sea again.

To brands of that stature, internationalism blends into global-ism. Sheer size brings resources, access and power that others don't have – and it enables brand development to blend with politics and diplomacy. After typical '49% solutions' to develop Coca-Cola's in-terests in the US and the Far East, the collapse of the Soviet Bloc en-abled Goizueta and Ivester to bring their manic focus to bear on the global development of the brand on an unprecedented scale.

It didn't matter if Pepsi wasn't present. It didn't matter if they already had a huge market share. Their challenge became one of growing the overall market – which partly involved pinching mar-ket share from the local soft drinks and partly, on occasion, becom-ing a macro-economic wealth-creating agent for the region. Huge investments were agreed for Eastern Europe – mostly in distribu-tion and bottling facilities, but sometimes in the basic infrastructures needed to service and support them. Major currency risks were un-dertaken. Much of this was not done on a business-to-business basis (B2B), as would normally be the case. It was done on a business-to-government basis – that B2G dimension open only to a handful of the world's great brand names. Few have used it more effectively than Goizueta at this time and in these places.

Zeitgeist marketing

We noted Coca-Cola's loss of market positioning and relevance in the late 1970s and early 1980s. Pepsi did to Coca-Cola what punk rock did to the Moody Blues. It signalled a new energy and a re-jection of the staid and predictable Norman Rockwell-style old (or older) values. To some degree, Coca-Cola is suffering again as I write this in 2001, being tossed around on the surf of another counter-force. This time, the equivalent of the Sex Pistols are singing a song of anti-globalism.

In between, coinciding with the bulk of Goizueta's time on the bridge of the ship, Coca-Cola experienced a Golden Age of brand positioning.

In the 1980s America was more than just the free world's friend. It was their protector and, in many cases, their route (via the huge US market) to wealth creation. As the world became a global media village, the benign Americanisation of the planet gathered strength. I was amazed during my trips to (for example) Japan at just how much the post-Boomer generation celebrated everything American – from food to sporting heroes, from clothes to rock stars. The US championed freedom, the good life, and diversity. Coca-Cola hopped on for a ride.

Ironically, the seeds of the renaissance were sown in the dark years of the 1970s when a multi-ethnic group of youngsters assembled on a hillside and sang: 'I'd like to teach the world to sing, in perfect harmony. I'd like to buy the world a Coke, and keep it company'. Substitute 'sell' for 'buy' and that is exactly what happened, with an accelerating curve, during Goizueta's time. For a period, the US, by and large, basked in a sunny international image. It was welcome in most places by most people. When Coca-Cola spent millions on simple lines like 'The Real Thing' and 'Coke Is It', the *Thing* and the *It* were essentially America. Goizueta elevated this Brand Diplomacy approach to marketing to new heights, by turning the 1996 Atlanta Olympic Games, that highly prized showcase for a nation, into a highly expensive showcase for Coke. He wanted it to be one and the same thing.

When Douglas Ivester took over from Goizueta, it seems he contributed some self-inflicted wounds to the cause of his rapid downfall. In fairness, he also experienced some unlucky breaks – one of them being a climactic change in the attitude towards America as a (now solo) superpower, and a growing concern about the potential negatives around corporate globalism. More often than not, the great and successful ride a bit of luck as well.

Put the bullets where the Indians are

This is an appallingly racist and insensitive statement by some modern standards of political correctness, and I should know better. My childhood, however, was dotted with visits to the Saturday morning cinema, yelling support for the cowboys against the Indians. I could not begin to count the cavalry rescues I have cheered, or the surrounded wagon trains with which I have shared the agonies of impending doom. The influences went in deeply, and it was no surprise when I took over a big job about thirty years later that a piece of advice given to me by a wizened veteran of the UK brewing industry struck home. He told me not to waste my ammunition. He told me to put the bullets where the Indians are. If Bass Brewers were my fiercest competition, then I should concentrate my ammunition – my energy and resources – on damaging them.

I think the above conversation took place in Nottingham, in the English midlands, and I'm sure that there were only two people present in the room. It was still some years before Goizueta took over the reins at Coca-Cola, but he acts as though he was there in the room with the two of us, listening intently to my mentor, and taking notes. His blinkered approach to kicking Pepsi in the *cojones* at every available opportunity is a critical element in his formula for manic focus. He sent bullet after bullet towards those particular Indians.

A small percentage of business leaders ignore their competition. Their maxim is to let the opposition worry about them. Others, probably a majority, talk cheaply about knowing their competition, and it's usually superficial drivel – not much more than you can glean from half an hour with their published accounts and a Web browser. Some do take competition very seriously – I remember working with a big, branded yoghurt company who brought the company's senior management together with the sole purpose of attempting to write their key competitor's business plan. That degree of focus, however, is the exception rather than the rule. Most companies are not prepared to invest the time, resources and deflection needed to *really* get inside their competitor's heads. It's only when you are that besotted, however, that you get to do real damage.

Pepsi was much more than just a *bête noir* to Goizueta. His mood was never blacker than when he was losing to them, and he was never happier than when he momentarily allowed his gentlemanly exterior to be penetrated by a gloat over some market victory over his arch rival. Diet Coke (see below), which had been tried and aborted before Goizueta's time, was brought back by him, and given the Full Monty, in response to Pepsi's successful Diet Pepsi. I am also convinced that this fanatic focus on the 'Indians' drove much of Coke's east European game plan in the early 1990s. In a region of the world that had previously been a Pepsi stronghold, by 1992 every country except Czechoslovakia and Poland evidenced Coca-Cola with a leading market share. Those two countries would soon join the club.

The example that illustrates this single-mindedness best, however, is Venezuela. I watched this gladiatorial conflict with a personal interest. At the centre of it was the Cisneros family, who had been our Burger King franchisees in Venezuela. They were also Pepsi bottlers, and because of this Venezuela was one of the few countries in the world that did not switch when we moved the brand to Coca-Cola in the early 1990s.

This was not just the pursuit of another 49% solution. It was a Latin country, and the Cisneros family, like Goizueta, had Cuban roots. A personal friendship had developed between Roger Enrico, Goizueta's counterpart at Pepsi, and the Cisneros family, and there is no doubt that something personal overlaid all this. After the New Coke debacle (see below), Enrico pissed off Goizueta with his amusingly titled: *The Other Guy Blinked: How Pepsi Won The Cola Wars*,[3] and I suspect the latter had the former personally in the cross hairs in this particular theatre of war.

---

[3] An old saying has it that if you shoot a King, you must make sure he is dead. Was that ever true in that in this case …

Goizueta began stalking the Cisneros in 1994, and finally pulled of this huge coup in 1996 by acquiring 50% of the Venezuelan bottler. 2500 Pepsi branded trucks were over-painted with Coca-Cola. The deal was inked just after Enrico became Pepsi's CEO after a spell in their food operations, but he was too late to do anything other than squeal. There is a saying in my native Lancashire that a very happy man is like a dog with a tin dick. I do not know if that translates into Spanish. If it does, I believe it could have been used to describe Roberto on this happy occasion.

There is one more intriguing element to Goizueta befitting from his focus on Pepsi. We will learn shortly that he was tempted twice to dilute his manic focus on his core product. Both ventures proved to be mistakes. For all we know, he may have been tempted to diversify on other occasions, and if he was I suspect it might have been a quick look at his key competition that caused him to back off. Pepsi's involvement in the highly capital-intensive, chain-restaurant and snack-food businesses has had its good times. More often than not it has left them with multi and confused priorities. They suffered as a result, particularly when they shared the ring with the Master of Manic Focus.

Ring the last drop out of your name

In Burger King, we had another powerful brand. It sold 2 million units *a day*. It had huge brand awareness, but we gave it no direct support. It was, and is still, called the Whopper, the brand's flagship sandwich.

Is there a conflict between the Whopper and Burger King? Should the *sandwich* have been called The Burger King, so that a unit of money spent supporting one would also support the other?

Coca-Cola had a diet drink – called Tab, remember? – in the fast-growing, diet-drink market of the early 1980s. Within days of Goizueta's gaining power, an ambitious young marketer called Sergio Zyman thoughtfully resurrected an old project of the new master. Tab wasn't doing well against the new Diet Pepsi, and a new product launch was proposed. By calling the proposed new brand Diet Coke, it would be an *extension* of the Coca-Cola brand, it would provide bottlers with a much-needed new product, and it would go head to head with Diet Pepsi in a way that Tab would not do.

The rest is history. It was a silver bullet for Goizueta. By the end of 1983, within 18 months or so of Goizueta's coronation, Diet Coke was the best selling diet drink in the US – and within another year it had climbed to number three in the entire soft drink market. Tab withered and died on the vine.

I have listed six different elements that illustrate how Goizueta focussed on Coca-Cola. Together they add up to Manic Focus. Jointly and severally, they enabled him to take a brand that many thought was tired and possibly past its shelf life, and revitalise it. In doing so, he delivered one of the biggest Dreams on record.

There is one further dimension for us to consider, and it is a strange one. I have called it the Power of a Mistake.

There is a difference between a mistake and a failure, but the paranoia of modern business is such that we've forgotten how to differentiate between the two. You should not survive failure. If you have the correct delegation of accountability and responsibility, a failure should see you fired. A mistake, however, is something you not only survive, but something that facilitates progress. *It is a catalyst.* You may go one step back, but you can then go two steps forward, simply by learning from what doesn't work and avoiding repetition.

I am not going to document the rise and fall of New Coke in any detail. It has been done extensively – enough to put it on any list of the most high profile (and expensive) balls-ups in history. What I am going to do is look at the role New Coke played in the triumph of Coca-Cola at the turn of the millennium.

Historian Barbara Tuchman, in her magnificent opus *The March Of Folly*,[4] had a way of defining 'mistakes'. Roaming over some of

---

[4] Ballantine Books, 1984.

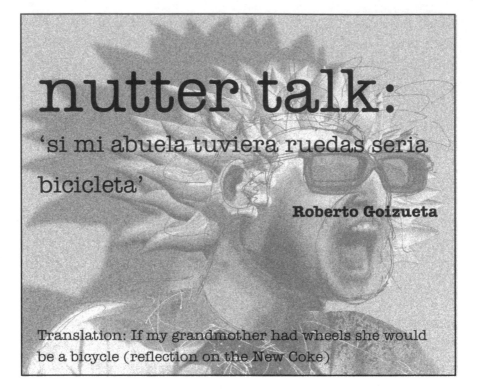

nutter talk:

'si mi abuela tuviera ruedas seria bicicleta'

Roberto Goizueta

Translation: If my grandmother had wheels she would be a bicycle (reflection on the New Coke)

history's finest, from Troy to Vietnam, she 'graded' them by working out their 'fully costed' consequences. By this method, one of the greatest mistakes ever made was the decision, taken by the Germans, to resume unrestricted submarine warfare in 1916. After a time-out following the Lusitania nightmare, this meant that all shipping – military, merchant or civil – was re-targeted. Here's the high speed version of what happened as a consequence: America joined the war, the drift towards an uneasy peace was shattered, the impasse was broken, the Allies won, reparations followed, Hitler thrived, the second world war happened. Now *that's* a mistake.

Judged on these criteria – i.e. the sum of the negative consequences – I advocate that New Coke was the smallest mistake in history. Sure it cost money, but look what happened to Coke's stock value over Goizueta's reign. The research behind New Coke was flawed, focussing on attitudinal response to the new product and forgetting to ask what the customer attitude would be if the new cola were accompanied by the withdrawal of the existing iconic brand.

The 'fully costed' consequences bear thinking about. If ever Goizueta had doubts about the need for manic focus, this episode must have removed them. *After New Coke he knew he had no choice.* There could never be a 'new improved' product. There could never be a Coke equivalent of 'Windows 98'. The product was untouchable. *That kind of information is priceless.* At a stroke it removes a ton of options, and facilitates manic focus.

In parallel, Goizueta made another strategic error that provided him with the same kind of mind-benefit. In an early attempt to de-risk the company's reliance on what was still perceived to be a struggling brand, Goizueta acquired Columbia Pictures in 1982. Again, this story has commanded more than enough narrative, so a simple summary will suffice here. By 1989 Goizueta wanted out. The issues of management and capital deflection, plus the complications around the increasing need to 'censure' movies with non-Coca-Cola like material made it a headache. The skills needed for the two businesses were incompatible. Coca-Cola actually lost money on the successful *Gandhi,* and lost a whole bucketful more on one of the great box-office bombs of all time, *Ishtar.*

Movies were too unpredictable for Goizueta, and he put the thing on the block. Not infrequently his brilliance was helped by a bit of luck, and good fortune smiled on him again. Someone massively overpaid him to take Columbia Pictures off his hands, and he bagged a handsome profit for Coke's increasingly smiling investors.

The lesson of new Coke was hammered home again. Coca-Cola was the only game in town. In the words of the Eagles: *There was no new frontier. He would have to make it here.*

This manic focus involved a massive pyramid of supporting activities such as the resurrection of the famous five-cent bottle shape. The results of Manic Focus were impressive. Roberto Goizueta lived to see the Guinness Book Of Business Records list Coca-Cola as the most powerful brand, simultaneously, in Europe, the USA, the UK and the world.

That is some Dream, and he is some Dream Merchant. His style is not that of a highly distinctive HowBoy, however. The man with whom I shared a one-hour flight that evening in the early 1990s gave the impression that he was as happy off-stage as on it. Manically focussed, determined, consistent and visionary – you would never question his power or control. It was, however, largely hidden behind his fascia of old Cuban charm and grace. You found yourself lowering your voice to talk back to him. One to one, I didn't find him inspiring in the way, say, Tony O'Reilly could leave you feeling recharged after ten minutes with him. Goizueta was not an extrovert and he wasn't 'rah-rah'. His leadership style did not include Branson-style abseiling down the outside of buildings.

It was what he did, not how he did it, that buzzes around my memory. What he did was up there with the best of them

NUTTER SCORE:

Dream Merchant: Five stars (plus merit)

HowBoy: Two stars

TRIBUTE TO THE
UNKNOWN NUTTER

10

I'M THROWING A STRANGE CHAPTER IN HERE. At the outset of this book, I emphasised that, along with a bit of entertainment and the passing on of some useful ammunition in the event you need to impress somebody, the purpose of this book was to see what some celebrity Nutters had done that we could use.

Our own journey's are, of course, much more mundane. It is unlikely that anyone reading this book will shortly lead the world into a new age of communication, or reinvent branding, or build a Disneyland, or pull off the world's biggest industrial merger. Indeed, the odds are against anyone reading this book ever being in the *close company* of such an icon.

Our journeys are more likely to involve starting up a small business or running a small team or business unit. They may, or may not, include the pleasures of having 'subordinates' reporting to you. You may or may not have your own money on the line. Foreign markets and globalisation may bring back fading memories of school geography lessons, but be of no more relevance to your day-to-day grind. The world's business media may be continuing to show precisely sod-all interest in your opinion on anyone or anything. Your boss may, or may not, be a cross between a mental spastic and an intellectual midget, neatly defined by me in one of my lesser moments as a *spidget*. You would not know a private jet if it bit you in the groin. Seven figure bonuses and squillions of share options have mysteriously passed you by. A Fat Cat you are not.

You continue, however, to do your thing. You have some ambitions, and you have pride. You would like whatever it is you are doing NOW to be a success – partly for the rewards, partly for the kudos and partly because it might lead to greater things. I just bet you could handle a successful Dream if it happened to you.

When I have performed a sort of field surgery on these Dream Merchants and HowBoys, I have tried to entertain and educate – but also to filter off the stuff that worked for them and *might work for you.*

Some of the principles are, I am convinced, transferable – and it is worth remembering that all – I repeat *all* – of these folk started out on the bottom rung. Not one of these people, all of whom have recorded successes that will see them etched into the History Of Business, had their success handed to them on a plate. None of them were deflected by the constant vomiting caused by having a silver spoon stuck in their mouth.

In the last chapter of the book, I will draw all this together to see if we can get some of this stuff in a transferable state for you to use next week. In this chapter, however, I am going off at a tangent.

It is 37 years since I sat at my first office desk for something other than a holiday job. The honour of hosting my corporate debut fell to Shell-Mex and BP Ltd, a joint marketing company set up by those two oil giants in the UK. I joined their Manchester office. From then on until 1994, punctuated by two breaks to get university degrees I neither needed nor used, I occupied a series of increasingly posh, and more and more unlikely, desks. I worked for three great companies, and the journey through the three of them exposed me to business in about 50 countries. It also exposed me to a handful of Nutters who would never make a list like the contents page of this book. Few in business had heard of them at the time, and few since.

Somehow, however, they stuck in my mind. Now *that*, according to my family, is a strange place to be stuck. It retains megabytes of essential information such as the name of the bass guitarist of the Searchers pop group (c.1964),[1] but forgets completely somebody I met yesterday.

Somehow, the folk and the events in this chapter were stored on my mental hard drive, just waiting for the correct time and circumstances for retrieval. It is here, and it is now. I have changed no names – I admire them all and if I am not complimentary, I will have failed in my articulation. They are all unknown Nutters, and there are lessons here for all of us.

I'm going to talk about only three such cases in this chapter, although the temptation was there to multiply that several times. Both Dream Merchants and HowBoys exist in this atmosphere, the former rather surprisingly, but what I have done is to omit the dickheads. We all know somebody who is the Office Nutter, who dresses oddly and/or behaves a bit weirdly at work – but any superficial analysis shows this to be a result of some genetic or mental defect. We need to avoid the attention seekers, the extroverts, the drunkards, the sexually inadequate and the reality-TV wannabes.[2] Surprisingly, when we chop all of them out, there are some genuine mavericks who can teach us a thing or two, despite never having a personal net worth in excess of a billion.

I'll start in, I think, 1978. I had left Shell for Whitbread PLC, and been appointed to run their East Midlands region. My responsibili-

---

[1] Tony Jackson.
[2] Occasionally, and regrettably, I have taken up some of these roles. I said SOME.

ties included the warehousing, sale and distribution of beer, wines and spirits to the tenanted, free and managed pubs and clubs within my designated bit of God's earth. It included Leicester, the City that God Forgot.

The warehousing and distribution side of our business reflected a much wider battle going on in British business and society – the fight between unions and management. British labour relations were crappo, and worsening by the day – although little did we (the management) know that salvation was just around the corner in the form of Mrs. Thatcher who effectively neutered a generation of shop stewards by crushing their 'nads between two blue handbags.

Such entertainment still lay in the future, and I conducted my daily management task effectively on tiptoe. Our depot shop steward was a card-carrying communist, and his contribution to a new world order was to whinge like a dentist's drill at anything and everything that threatened the *status quo* or the guaranteed overtime of his members. Looking back, it is not unfair to say that day-to-day business was like that famous football match that took place between German and British troops in no-man's land during a lull in the fighting in the Great War. It was a short break for sanity, then it was back to the business of trying to slaughter each other.

I had, however, a secret weapon. His name was Dick Hardingham, and he managed the warehouse, the trucks, and workforce that operated both. He was young in relative terms for a front-line 'industrial relations' position, but had served his apprenticeship in one of the tougher Theatres Of War – Liverpool.

For some reason he found himself heading home early one day – which, for him, involved a drive across country. It was about 2 pm, and he passed one of those quaint self-service operations that dot the British countryside – Pick Your Own Strawberries. He was in a hurry to get home – if my memory is correct he had a commitment to go somewhere with his wife and was already late. So, let's just say he was travelling at speed, but not fast enough for him to miss three big vehicles, parked up, with their drivers constructively employed picking strawberries. The three vehicles were our company's delivery trucks, with our logo in huge letters on the sides and back. They were out on a day's deliveries, and not due back to the depot until about 5 pm.

He couldn't, and didn't stop. He arrived home half an hour later, and proceeded to get ready to go out. It was no use. I have no record of the conversation he had with his wife (although I can imagine), but it surely had a lot of expletives in it, probably from both sides. It ended with him jumping back into his car and returning to the depot. All the trucks were parked, with the drivers in the locker-room. I would ask you again to remember the industrial relations climate of the day, as he did when he approached the Whinge-Wizard (our shop steward) to draw his attention to the fact that three of 'his' crews had been strawberry picking on company time, while being paid company money and generating company overtime.

He got his complaint batted straight back at him – all the trucks were back, all the beer delivered. What was the problem? If he hadn't taken the time to deal with it at the time, at the field, there was no proof of a misdemeanour and, therefore, no grounds for a disciplinary action. So there.

With a cry of 'Bollocks to that', Dick walked straight past him, into the locker room, stood by the door, told everybody to file out past him, *and to hold out their hands.* Given the industrial relations background, this was hugely risky. It bore no relation to any known procedure. Had the climate in that room been one degree colder, the lot of them might have walked off the job then and there. The Whinge-Wizard was dancing about as though he had a viper down his trousers. There was something about Dick's square jaw, however, and something about the time and place, which all came together, and they just sheepishly did as they were told. There were six guys whose hands looked as though they had been marinated in beetroot for two days. Gotcha.

Dick got away with it. The rest of the guys started laughing and the culprits soon joined in and took their 'formal oral' warning in good heart. Our shop steward disappeared into the lavatory with his copy of *Das Kapital* trying to find a precedent or some operating instructions, and decided to bring down the government on another day.

There are two forces at work in this example of an unknown HowBoy at work. On it's own, the difference between right and wrong – and the selection of, and commitment to, the former – is powerful. It doesn't have to be against the background of a powder keg industrial relations climate. It doesn't have to be a moral or ethical right or wrong – it can simply be about the colour of the widget your team is developing. If you believe something passes what I call the *Test of Rightness*, then it has a built-in momentum with you. It empowers you to go to places you wouldn't normally go to. Others see you taking risks, but you don't see them as risks. You are suddenly surefooted and confident, in an area that your peers see as a minefield. If you genuinely believe something is right, there is a force with you that may cause you to surprise yourself.

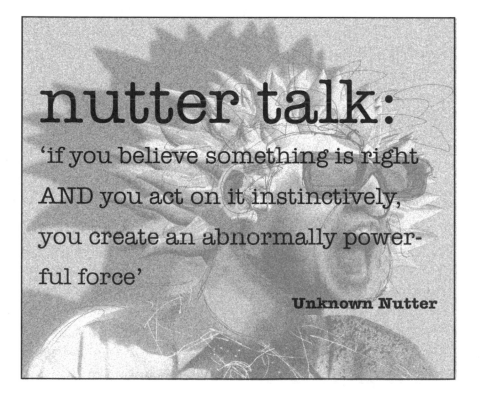

nutter talk:
'if you believe something is right AND you act on it instinctively, you create an abnormally powerful force'

Unknown Nutter

There is another natural force, which is also free, that you can harness. It is a force that is in danger of atrophy in modern corporate life – that of *acting on instinct*. We live, of course, in the information age – and the sheer speed with which we can access previously undreamed of amounts of data has been trumpeted as improving both the pace and quality of decision making. In my observation, that is Imperial Bollocks.

What the Information Age has done is give a whole generation of decision-takers reasons to procrastinate. There is always another analysis possible, always another 'what-if' loop you can run through the model. Many (most?) corporate decisions are now being taken by a combination of software and the company lawyer – the software printing out the model options, and the lawyer telling you the one with the least risk.

The idea of a leader digesting a set of circumstances, and taking action then and there, backed only by his or her instincts, causes business school professors and lawyers to wear incontinence pads. But it can be so, SO powerful – for the simple reasons that your competitors can match your software, and they can pay their lawyers more than you pay yours – but they can't match your instinct.

There are two forces listed above. The momentum coming from a belief *something is right*, and the power of occasionally *acting on instinct*. What Dick Hardingham did was fuse the two together. Now, if you can do that, it is real Star Trek stuff, because it can take you where no man has been before. Or, at least, to where you haven't. It doesn't matter where you are in the food chain, if you can bring these two forces to bear on occasion, it can get you through barriers and break deadlocks – at *your* level, and *for you*. The combination creates an abnormally positive force.

My second example is so 'unknown' that I can't remember his surname. Coincidentally, the timing was around the same as my first example, and the location involved the same piece of geography.

As part of our business in Whitbread, we sold and delivered beer to the big workingmen's clubs of the east Midlands. This region had a heritage of coal mining, and these guys drank beer in copious quantities. Much of their social life was centred on work-associated 'clubs', which provided recreation and frequent entertainment. At their peak, the extensive memberships of these clubs, and the sheer size of their beer revenues, enabled them to book big-budget international stars and, for a while, they delayed the death of big-time live variety in the UK.

The beer business in these places was often of a size that meant it had to be supplied in *tanks* rather than in conventional kegs, and was a very competitive business. We did well, on balance winning more of these big accounts than we lost, but after a few months there was one characteristic in the marketplace that began to intrigue me more and more. One of our competitors *never* lost an account once they had it.

There were about ten beer companies fighting it out, and the one with this unusual characteristic was Bass. I got to know most of the key guys in our competitors, and eventually shared a coffee with the 'key account' manager for Bass. I'm still not sure whether it was by accident or design, but he told me of a ritual that had been put in place by the company's veteran Free Trade Sales Director that (indirectly) explained everything.

The Director's name was James something, and he smoked a pipe. That's all I can remember of this shadowy Nutter, although I met him a few times afterwards, and can see him clearly in my mind's eye. He was based, with his regional Board, at Burton on Trent, the heartland of Bass's extensive UK operations. Here's the deal he put in place: if any salesman, or woman, *lost an account*, they were required to attend the next Board meeting, in person, and explain why. It would then be discussed (and minuted), and the poor bastard would then return to the trenches, ostensibly without a stain on his or her corporate character. Yeah, right.

The process was not billed as a disciplinary or negative thing. It was billed as a way of keeping the Board in touch with what was going on in the marketplace, and was a very effective way of doing

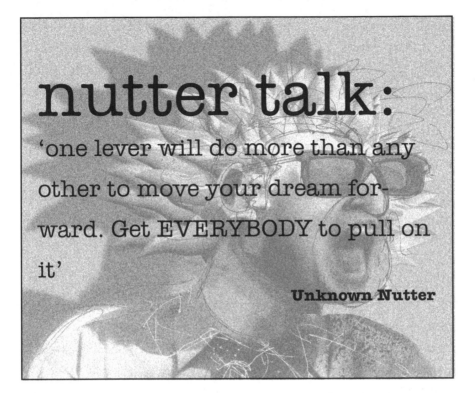

nutter talk:

'one lever will do more than any other to move your dream forward. Get EVERYBODY to pull on it'

Unknown Nutter

so. But can you imagine what it seemed like to a young, ambitious salesperson? You had to dress up, and drive to Burton and parade yourself in front of these company icons, with the Board secretary studiously recording what a wanker you had been. It took me about ten minutes to figure out that James was only partially interested in the information he got out of these sessions. His main priority was exactly that which he effectively achieved – his team *dreaded* losing an account. You know what happened as a result? You couldn't win an account off these guys at any price. They defended them as though they were defending their children from a predator. They fought cleanly, and if that didn't work they hit below the belt. They did whatever it took to avoid that dreaded journey to Burton.

More sophisticated gurus, and more sophisticated analysts than James have arrived at the same conclusion that he got to, I suspect, using a hunch and personal experience. It is far, far more effective and efficient to keep and grow your *existing* business than to be constantly winning and losing accounts. The efficacy of the actual practice, however, is not why he is here. What I loved about this unknown Nutter is that, with *one* procedure, he crystallised a goal and made sure everybody in the team had a vested interest in dealing with that as the first item on their agenda every day.

James wasn't just about focus and priority. It was more than that – it was about leverage. In any project, challenge or Dream building, there will be some activities that are miles more effective than others in getting the job done. Identifying that is one thing. Articulating the rhetoric to make it a hunting call for all involved is another. To then invent a way to get your team to personally sweat for it is magnificent.

I don't think this barmy old bugger paid any attention to any of the jittery boardroom presentations put in front of him. That was never the point. It didn't matter anyway – after a year or so there weren't any account losses to report. Quaint and weird he may have been, but pound for pound I have never faced a tougher competitor, and I have never forgotten him.

My third example couldn't be more different. Although (largely) unknown in business circles, he has achieved fame in his chosen career – that of a soccer manager.

During the 1980s, Dave 'Harry' Bassett took Wimbledon on an unlikely fairytale journey from non-league soccer to the top league in the English professional game. Around 1987, I had moved on from Whitbread, and was running a division of GrandMet called the Host Group, which consisted of around 1600 directly-managed pubs and restaurants. I was planning a management conference. I had inherited the chief executive's job from a guy who did more damage to the British pub industry than the Luftwaffe ever managed. He had been given a mandate to spend huge amounts of capital in an attempt to drag the UK pub business into the twentieth century, and had spent it. Mostly badly. I inherited a number of negative results from the programme, one being that the culture of the company reflected an attitude that growth only came if you bought it.

One of the goals of the conference I was planning was, therefore, to refocus on organic growth. I needed to drive home the idea that you could nurture what you had and get your existing customers to come more often and spend more with you than the competition. As we were planning the conference, I heard on the grapevine that 'Harry' was interested in doing some professional motivational speaking, and we met up to explore the idea.

He was (and still is) a Max Miller-type 'cheeky-chappie-Londoner' – which hides a shrewd and thoughtful side to his personality that the public rarely sees. He impressed me immediately with a piece of crystallised, homespun wisdom that was exactly what I needed, and why he is in this chapter. We agreed that he would build a 30-minute speech around it, and that it would be the keynote speech to our conference. I will share it with you in a moment, and it is powerful – but first I must tell you how the day panned out. You seem in need of some light relief, and I smile to this day at its recollection.

The stage was set – literally – for the day with two lecterns, one at each side. I was ever-present on stage, doing my bits and then staying quiet while others did theirs at the other lectern. Most of us used autocue, which is a facility that enables the speech-giver to 'read' from a thin, transparent screen in front of him or her, which is angled so that the audience cannot see it. The technology that enables that is relatively simple – a TV monitor is located, facing upwards, in the bottom of the lectern, and the contents of that screen are reflected onto the screen in front of the speaker. An autocue operative will normally scroll your speech in time with your own voice – so you read it as it comes up. If you don't want to speak verbatim, you can have notes or bullet points scrolled up.

Harry was not comfortable with reading from the autocue, so we agreed we would put his bullet-points on it. Time management was important as we had a full day, and we needed him to stay

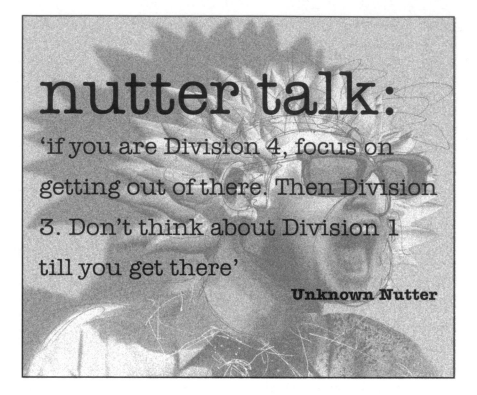

nutter talk:

'if you are Division 4, focus on getting out of there. Then Division 3. Don't think about Division 1 till you get there'

Unknown Nutter

within some structure. All that planning, however, went for a ball of chalk as he strolled on after my introduction, smiled at the rapturous applause, and threw his notes down on the upward-facing TV screen in the bottom of the lectern. His autocue obviously went blank as a result. He blinked once, but was otherwise not thrown at all by this development. He set off on his speech with enthusiasm, and no guidance.

After about 25 of his allotted 30 minutes, it was clear we were off-mission. Wimbledon had just got out of the Fourth Division, and we were stuck for some time on the problems of his centre forward's troublesome cartilage injury. My longed-for words of wisdom were nowhere in sight.

I was not too bothered. Frankly, these events are mostly about finding creative ways to justify tax-relief for a piss-up in the evening, and the audience had settled back and were lapping it up. My producer, however, was less relaxed and started sending messages to Harry on the autocue system – sort of: '*5 mins to go, Harry, start to wind up'*. Now, I could receive them, and I did. Harry, of course, couldn't – but the producer didn't know that.

There then followed an escalating series of messages from the producer to the completely unknowing Harry. As we passed the 45-minute mark, they began appearing in coloured fonts, and bouncing up and down. I lost all interest in the chronology of the day, and just celebrated each new message as it beamed up to me but not the target. My stomach began to ache as I tried to suppress my laughter. Expletives began to appear after an hour, and we were STILL having problems with Fashanu's knee.

Eventually, a message appeared in which every letter was in a different colour, and underlined. It was simple. It read: '*HARRY – GET THE FUCK OFF STAGE. NOW NOW NOW.*' It began to bounce up and down on the screen. I couldn't handle it. With tears in my eyes, I ambled across the stage (to some mild booing) and brought to a close one of the finest pieces of modern oratory on record.

Oh dear. Where were we? His what? Oh, yes, his wisdom. It is powerful in its simplicity – particularly for those who seem a long way away from the sort of successes noted elsewhere in this book. Quite simply, he and his Wimbledon team never thought about the end point of the Dream, which turned out to be the English First Division. That's what eventually happened, but the Dream was made up of sub-dreams. When they were in the Fourth Division, *their whole focus was on getting out of there*. That's what they planned, resourced and trained for. When they got promoted, they turned their attention to the Third Division. When it didn't work (one year they slipped back down), they re-geared mentally to get back out again. *The only time they thought about the First Division was when they were in it.*

This is not, of course, the Steve Jobs approach to Dream building – he saw the equivalent of the First Division from Day One, and never really focussed on anything else. For those of us who don't have a vision like that, and we don't quite know what or where the end could be, Harry's Way might offer a practical alternative that we could start on next Monday.

So endeth my tribute to three unknown Nutters. I could have dredged up another 100 from my own odyssey. I make no apology in including them in such august company, because they are just as entertaining as some of the Big Guys, and the lessons learned can be just as relevant for us. Maybe more so.

STEVE JOBS

THERE ARE TWO SOCCER TEAMS IN MANCHESTER, England, just as there are two baseball teams in Chicago, Illinois. There are some strange similarities between the two pairs. In both cities, one of the two teams is successful, one isn't. The one that isn't successful, is spectacularly not so. It would be easy, the rational among you would think, for those 'fans' that follow the team with the lesser success, to switch allegiance. My reply to you, if you are one of those 'wise' people, is that it is not difficult. It is impossible. I know.

I happen to follow Manchester City, and I agree it is possible that they have had more relative success than the Chicago Cubs have had over the last 100 years. It doesn't matter, our record is still crappo. As a mildly annoying contrast, across the city of Manchester,[1] Manchester United is possibly the most successful soccer club side of modern times. Every week, whether it is in season or not, wherever I am in the world, I scour the media and the Web for news of my side, and all I usually get is the glory of the other bastards.

Now then (and this is going somewhere, I promise), I am 55 years old and bright enough to have run a big company. In most other dimensions of life, certainly those measurable by conventional success criteria, I have scored reasonably. So why don't I just switch allegiance? My father, who is smiling down on all this from his final resting place, who took me to the City ground to watch my first game, is no longer here to frown at any betrayal. My family would be relieved. *Nobody need actually know.* It would make my life so much more fun. Sorry. I know I am an idiot, but it just isn't possible.

About four or five years ago, in America, I noticed a colleague, female as it happens, wrestling with an Apple software upgrade. Having never used Apple's operating system, I berated her for not being PC/IBM compatible. I got no words in reply, but I recognised that look I got in return. I had seen it in my own shaving mirror many times.

Apple is the computing world's equivalent of Manchester City. It triggers loyalty like Liquid Nails glue, and the worse the state it's in, the firmer the hold on its fan base.

It is, of course, inextricably linked with one man – Steve Jobs. This modern day equivalent of P. T. Barnum is in this collection because I now want to look at two elements of Dream making and HowBoyship that we haven't encountered so far – first, is it possible to *market* your way to a Dream? When we've looked at that, there's a second dimension to this guy's story that might have relevance for we lesser mortals: *just how high can you rise after you've been declared dead?*

---

[1] Some of us, who are desperate for any high ground, would argue that it was in an adjacent city, and not in Manchester at all.

A couple of years ago, *Business Week* magazine included Jobs in the list of their annual top executives. He was, at the time, riding the success of the iMac and PowerBook personal computers. The magazine lists awards for different categories of business leader, and they named him as a *marketer*, not a technocrat – although the business he ran competed in the high technology world of personal computing. They were absolutely right to do so.

I remember a comedy routine from about 15 years ago by Jasper Carrot, a rather demented comedian from the English midlands. He joked that he left school with only two 'O' levels[2] – one in Art and the other in Maths. With a deadpan expression, he delivered his punch line – that he then got a job painting computers.

If anybody challenges you to summarise Jobs' Dream in two words, now you have them. He *painted computers.*

Consider this. He is immensely rich and successful. Apple is a powerful and respected brand in the PC world – having survived a quarter century of a roller-coaster ride. Its fan base is as loyal and daft as Manchester City's and all of the above has been achieved by a mix of smoke, mirrors and paint.

How can this be? Well, consider this also: Jobs' rarely matched his marketing with technology. The products he marketed were either late arriving or off specification. Sometimes both. On other occasions it was too good – the point being it never matched. He couldn't forecast his way out of a wet paper bag. For a long time he fought the wrong enemy (the PC hardware makers) with the wrong product (PC hardware). If it's any help to him, and he reads this, he still is. If there is genuine point of distinction about Apple, it is the operating system. Windows was the enemy, not IBM.

Ask people what they remember of the first of the two stints he had at Apple, and they will probably say it was an advert (the celebrated 1984 spot at the 1984 US Super Bowl). He was then drummed

---

[2] These are the external exams taken by 16 year olds in England – now called GCSEs. You would normally sit between five and ten.

out of the company, and it nearly died. He came back to rescue it. Ask the same people what they remember about the second coming, and they will probably recall all those nice pastel colours of the iMac. He painted the bloody things.

This is a born marketer.

Marketing, as a science, is vastly over-complicated by those who (usually) have a vested interest in over-complicating it. It revolves about the creation of distinction for a product or service. In theory, when you have that, you generate awareness of that distinction in your target market which, in turn, generates a trial purchase. After that the trick is to generate loyalty, and get the customer to spend more on the product/service – either by paying more, buying more or by buying more frequently.[3]

If that is the summary art or science of marketing, we are in the presence of a master, and maybe *the* contemporary master. So, let's look a little deeper, and see what makes a master-marketer. More to the point, let's see if there is anything we can steal.

The first thing any master-marketer (MM for short) demonstrates is distinction. Jesus, Gibbons, *you've just said that.* Aha, but wait! This is not distinction in the product or service; it is in the appearance and/or behaviour and/or personality of the MM himself or herself. They market *themselves* first and foremost.

If you go into any serious marketing agency, and talk to any account executive, I can guarantee you will not be in the presence of a 'grey' person. It doesn't have to a physical manifestation, although hairstyle, clothes and accessories can play an important part. What is critical is that you, the audience, very quickly receive signals that you are in the presence of some body that is quirky and odd. You then make the mental jump to the assumption that this person must possess this strange attribute you've head so much about, this thing called *creativity*. Once you get to that stage, the next level is relatively easy – you assume that this person is everything that you are not,

---

[3] If you are very clever, both.

and that you need to buy this talent. I've seen this achieved by a male carrying a handbag in England in the 1970s.

Branson's good at it, but he needs bigger and bigger props. If there is a better proponent of self-selling than Jobs over the last two decades, using just his own persona, then I am not aware of it. His personal brand equity is astonishing. But this is not an art, it is a science. I am quite convinced that every appearance is a studied and thought-through stage entrance, whether a formal stage is involved or not. From his 1975 appearance in front of a potential customer, BAREFOOT, to land a 50-computer deal, to the jeans and turtle neck uniform of the modern MM.

Incidentally, as a mildly interesting follow-on from the 50-computer deal, Jobs accepted the sale without having any idea how he was going to deliver the goods. They had no resources to produce and deliver such an order, and – as it turned out – a skill-gap. He eventually 'delivered' a batch of motherboards stuffed with components, *and got paid in full.* A powerful precedent was set here. Bullshit followed by non-delivery can work, and it has not made its last appearance in the Steve Jobs story.

There can be no doubt that MMs are profoundly more aesthetic that the norm. It follows on from their personal appearance, and now starts to involve what they do. The visual aspect of everything they associate with has to be just-so. There can be no compromise, and it means that style can frequently come to out-vote substance in what these people do. Style is a driving force with Jobs. In 1977, Apple shared an office in Cupertino, California, with Sony. Our hero was forever in the latter's office – not to try and steal technical secrets, but to look at their marketing materials, letterheads, logos – even the *weight* of their corporate notepaper.

It was Jobs who finalised the famous Apple logo design in 1977, and you thought it was simply a striped graphic apple with a bite out of it?

'One of the deep mysteries to me is our logo, the symbol of lust and knowledge, bitten into, all crossed with the colors of the rainbow in the wrong order. You couldn't dream of a more appropriate logo: lust, knowledge, hope and anarchy'

Jean-Louis Gassée

President, Apple Products[4]

Yup, these things are important. To an MM, a product is not a product, a service is not a service. They are works of art. Now, I am not making this next bit up. Since real artists sign their masterpieces, Jobs *had the signatures of the Macintosh team chemically etched on to the inside of the early Macs.*

In Jobs' journey, the triumph of style over substance has contributed to both the strengths and weaknesses, and the triumphs and the failures of Apple. I am typing this on a Compaq Presario. It is a boring, black, rectangular laptop. It bears no comparison to a funky Apple PowerBook, with its aesthetic shape and relevant colours, but it is Jobs' fanaticism about the looks of the box that have sown the seeds of Apple's eventual demise. The product he should have concentrated on, the one that had real, sustainable, distinction was never the box. It was the operating system. If he had concentrated on that, I would have been able to order my Compaq, or Dell (or whatever) with a choice of Windows' or Apple's operating system. Indeed, there are many who believe that if he had recognised that – and then concentrated his legendary skills upon marketing Apple's true core competence, Windows 95 might never have happened.

Today, his challenge is scary. The Apple operating system remains distinct, and the power and speed can be up there with the best of them. Which is precisely not the point. To keep these distinctions coming wrapped in expensive (both production and marketing cost are obviously higher than industry averages) but neat looking boxes is high risk. There are not many shapes and/or colours left.

---

[4] Quoted in *Apple Confidential*, Owen W. Linzmayer, Group West, 1999.

As well as being aesthetes, MMs have a hatred of elevator music. They abhor anything that has no impact. They would much rather someone hated their work, than that they had no opinion about it.

High impact is critical for these folk. You need high impact to change existing, or create new, behaviour in consumers – which is the goal of marketers. In the field of modern marketing, however, to achieve high impact is either difficult, or expensive or both. In previous generations you would take a deep breath, write a big cheque and you could guarantee reaching your target market via the limited media options open to you (and them). Not so now. The fragmentation of media, plus the explosion in the number of supported brand products, has meant the consumer is *nearly blind* in his or her ability to see and digest a brand message amidst the clutter they are exposed to everyday. To achieve impact, therefore, you have to cover a lot more media options that ever – a saturation bombing of the market. Or, you make what you do memorable, so that if it is seen it sticks in the mind.

The latter is cheaper, but it brings risks. To rise above the elevator music of modern brand marketing and create something memorable enough to change consumer attitude and behaviour to your product, MMs will normally choose one of two routes. One is humour, and (for example) Heineken in the UK in the 1970s and, more recently, the animated Budweiser campaigns (in the US) have scored via making 'em laugh. The alternative is usually to be controversial, and this book started with the master of controversy in Benetton's Toscani.

Jobs' famous advert, named *1984* after both the year of its launch and the George Orwell novel that it spoofed, was aimed at high impact. It combined high spend (with notoriously expensive US Super Bowl spots) and controversy. It positioned (although Jobs never formally admitted it) Apple as the freedom agent against the Big Brother of IBM. It was a magnificent example of what can be done by standing back and throwing a big brick at a still pond. The impact was phenomenal, even outside the US. It launched the Macintosh to a world that was suddenly convinced it wanted it – no, that it *needed* it. Recall scores for the advert were outrageous, and initial orders were of what Dreams are made.

However, not for the first time, nor the last, after the launch, the medium term sales missed forecast by miles. Apple couldn't deliver against the created imagery, and those who got one also acquired a load of technical SNAFUs. There is also an interesting sidebar. Jobs stated that the '1984' spot would never air again – but it did. Just enough to qualify it for the current year's advertising awards. Sometimes, with MMs, the success of marketing can be measured in other than the sales of the product. Winning the equivalent of a marketing Oscar can offset commercial failure. In this case it also had to offset Jobs subsequent firing from Apple – but it was a milestone in marketing history.

Blame for many of modern society's ills is directed at the fact we have no 'common' enemy. The theory being that if we have a Hitler, or some such, staring at us from across the English Channel, then our energies are organised and focused on this one cause. When we are so engaged (apparently – I wasn't there) then there is no drug abuse, teenage violence, road rage, profanity, under-age sex and yada yada yada. All complete bollocks of course, but it makes for a nice theory – and there is no doubt that having a common enemy helps focus. In particular, MMs love them.

There is something about being Burger King to a McDonalds, or Pepsi to a Coca-Cola that brings out the best in these folk. I loved having McDonalds as an enemy, particularly as they made a bunch of mistakes while I rode the other camel and made my life a lot easier. Punching the underbelly and kicking the ankles of a big bloated giant[5] brings the best out of MMs.

Jobs fought this imaginary head-to-head with IBM all his life, and I think is still fighting it. IBM were Coke to Apple's Pepsi – and

---

[5] This is always how you see them …

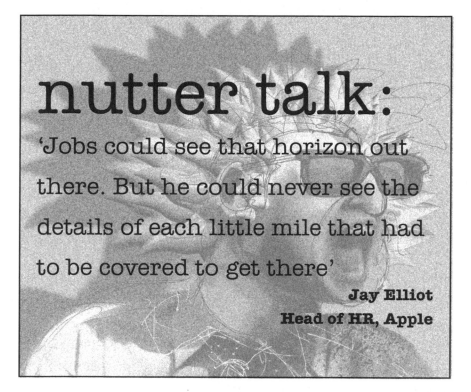

nutter talk:

'Jobs could see that horizon out there. But he could never see the details of each little mile that had to be covered to get there'

Jay Elliot
Head of HR, Apple

I refuse to believe it was a coincidence that he brought in John Sculley to head Apple. He was the man behind the successful Pepsi Challenge that dented Coke's armour in the late 1970s and early 1980s. In some ways it makes life easier to achieve high efficiency market impact if you can put two messages out there – how good your product is *and* how bad your competitor is.

1984 succeeded brilliantly as a piece of marketing, but the product never really backed it up. It was also, as we have noted, pointed at the wrong enemy. Even as early as the mid-1980s, it should have been Bill Gates in the cross hairs.

There is one last trait in these MMs that is worthy noting – they are, by and large, great showmen or showwomen. I was not totally joking at the start of this chapter when I likened Jobs to P. T. Barnum. Jobs has turned Apple into his personal Odyssey, and his personal showmanship has played a major part in his, and the company's

successes. He has a flair for the dramatic, often leaving the 'big' an-
nouncement right until the end of a presentation– then using it as a
throwaway. It is rarely that the world has seen its first sight of one of
his great designs without him cradling it personally. He will play to
the crowd, basking in his acclaim like the most accomplished diva.
He will stun a meeting with the unexpected – such as the introduction of Bill Gates, the arch-enemy of the late 1990s, via a satellite
link, suddenly as a friend and ally. When an actor played him in a
made-for-TV movie, which was not entirely complimentary, he quietly booked the actor for the next Apple event, and had him do the
first part of his presentation. He (the real Jobs) then walked on – to
silence, confusion, a dawning, and then HOWLING applause.

You can hate them for all this stuff. You can love them. You can
do both at once. You can scan it with the wisdom of 20-20 vision, and
point out the misdirection. You can do anything but ignore it, and
you can do anything but not be just a bit jealous. MMs are snake-oil
salesman, just working with bigger budgets and with bigger markets. They also entertain, and the best of them can keep going using
their magical smoke and mirrors long after they have no right to do
so.

I have no idea what Apple plans to be when it grows up (it's still
less than 30 years old). I have no idea whether it will reach middle
age. I suspect I am joined on both counts by Jobs. Whatever it is, and
if they make it, they have a chance if they can still draw on the skills
of this extraordinary painter of computers.

Before we leave Jobs, there is another aspect to his Dream making or HowBoyship that we should examine. *Just how dead do you
have to be to be dead?*

Since I left big business, I have been involved or acquainted
with a number of start-up businesses. Almost without exception,
they have all, at some time, been lying in a shallow grave, with a
sober group stood over them throwing earth down the hole. One
guy is usually muttering prayers. In fact, this usually happens every
month. The odd thing is that the entrepreneur involved in the start-

up simply will not die, and treats the pit-and-the-pendulum existence of a new company in the same way as he or she would clean
their teeth. It helps, of course, that they cannot die – because all they
have in the world (house, life-quality, family, marriage) often rests
on the eventual success of the venture, so it's best to just ignore the
obvious symptoms of death and get on with succeeding. Amazingly,
some of them come through, and it is this one-eyed resilience that
is a fundamental element in the success of the (reputed) 5% of new
starts that succeed.

That's unfair. It's more than just resilience. Faith and belief are
also in the mix. Somebody has to believe in the fucking thing, so
it may as well be you, the entrepreneur/owner. These people also
have an ability to provide and/or find resources, *somehow*, from cupboards that have long seemed empty, to meet another payroll or qui-
eten another unpaid vendor for another week.

Jobs' demise from, and comeback to, Apple are worth a closer
look. You can make cheap jokes about resurrections, but the story
has all the elements of the Big One – albeit with a happier ending for
a smaller number of people.

Apple began losing its way in the mid-1980s, and Jobs had just
the friend he needed in John Sculley, the man he had recruited from
Pepsi, to whack him in the 'nads just when he needed support. After
an astonishing semi-public arm wrestle between the two of them,
Jobs left, courtesy of a public letter of resignation.

It is wrong to assume that before his exit in 1985, Jobs was a
dictator at Apple. It was not a case of *l'état c'est moi*. Apple was a
public company, and had a very strong and powerful board – and
these wise men had already realised what Steve could, and couldn't,
do. Whatever formal or informal agreement he had with the board,
he was forever interfering where he shouldn't, and he and Sculley
ended up trying to pee in the same trough as they stared at piles of
unsold Macintoshes in 1985.

All that is written up elsewhere – the point being he had an acrimonious departure. We need to track both him and Apple quickly now for a decade or so, which they spent largely apart.

Apple recovered, and probably had a golden period in the early 1990s. By 1992, it had sold more individual computers than any other vendor worldwide, it was the most profitable personal computer company and had a cash reserve of $2 billion. Sculley, himself not a technocrat, was then deflected by a hand-held computer project, and allowed himself to be sucked into Clinton's run at the White House. Margins and profits slumped as the core product failed to compete against more cost effective 'commodity' PCs and Sculley jumped ship. He was aided by a $10 million severance package, but still messed it up, joining a serial loser called Spectrum.

In 1993, a guy called Michael Spindler replaced Sculley. The company floundered and was the subject of constant takeover and/or merger rumours. In 1995 Microsoft rewrote the rules by launching Windows 95, on the back of a humble $200 million budget. Ouch. Spindler gave way in 1996 to the renowned Gilbert F. Amelio, not surprisingly brought in as a company doctor. He arrived at the door of a company now low on cash, with poor quality products (the new ones hadn't delivered, the old ones were still on the vine) the development of its core competence (the operating system to fight Windows 95) was in disarray, there was no focus and the place was unmanageable.

Amelio has taken a lot of criticism, but there is *post facto* evidence that he knew what he had to do to stabilise things on all fronts. It's not that he didn't get the time, but that part of his solution was to acquire, within a year of his taking office, a software company that would support the development of its own new generation operating system. The acquired company was called NeXT, and it brought with it its founder and main shareholder, Steve Jobs.

It may have been a bold move, but it was also his death warrant. When he looked outside the Apple compound, he might have seen a familiar figure in jeans and turtleneck. It was actually a wooden horse.

Let's go back to the original 1985 divorce, and quickly trace what happened, in parallel, to Jobs. He failed to learn the Apple lesson, and tried to recreate a computer company, called NeXT – this time focussing on the education and business 'Rolls-Royce' PC market. Disaster. Now, the lesson was learned, albeit temporarily – and the hardware division of NeXT was ditched. Jobs concentrated on NEXTSTEP – targeted as a premium operating system for Intel-based computers.

In broad parallel with the NeXT journey, in 1986 Jobs invested $10 million for a majority interest in a company called Pixar, the computer division of George 'Star Wars' Lucas' film-making company. Around about 1995, not long after the hardware dream of NeXT had died, Jobs had forked out $50 million to keep Pixar going. At this time, we see Jobs at his lowest. Apple, his love child is in a real mess, and in the hands of a company doctor with a mandate to slash, burn and (probably) sell. He has long since left it. His two personal recovery vehicles are eating into his seed corn cash and, it seemed, going nowhere. The guy was dead. In fairness, he had built more of a Dream than you or I, but it was all over. Ashes to ashes.

Then, in 1995, Disney released *Toy Story* using Pixar animation technology. BOOM. On the back of it, Jobs offered some stock to the public. The closing price valued his remaining stock at more than $1 billion. In 1995 also, NeXT announced its first profit. Late in 1996, Apple acquired NeXT for $427 million and Jobs returned.

What happened next is more than well documented elsewhere, and only adds a foamy top to my main point. In 1997 Amelio resigned from Apple, having run up $1.6 billion in losses in a 17-month reign. Jobs took over, originally as a reluctant 'interim' CEO. iMac was launched, and in 1998 those painted computers sold at the rate of one every fifteen seconds. They were accompanied by a revised PowerBook. The NeXT software strategy was aborted (!) and a new generation of Mac OS was introduced to Manchester City – oops, sorry, – Apple OS lovers everywhere. By 1998, Apple was back in profit, with cash in the bank and less inventory than the famously lean and mean Dell Computers. Stores within stores opened at CompUSA, and the Cube – the desktop Apple – was on its way.

I'm stopping this story right here, because if I bring it up to date, it gets a bit gooey. Apple's back suffering again as I write, but my point here is this: has there been a more jet-like upward recovery by any single person (on this earth) than that experienced by this guy from 1995 –1998? He'd had a dream, maybe worthy of inclusion in this book by itself – and lost it completely. In a parallel universe to him, the Dream itself all but died. His post-first Dream world is going nowhere. Within three years, however, he's back in, painting computers again, and they are both alive and kicking and confounding the cynics on Wall Street and in the cut throat world of PCs.

We learn two big things from this study. First, this guy – maybe the greatest marketer alive – is a great dreamer. But I don't believe he is a great Dream Merchant, and seeing the difference may help us in our own quests. A Dream Merchant builds a sustainable dream, a test of which is how it survives without him or her.

I love this guy. He has added huge value to the growth of a complex new industry and created enormous wealth for himself and thousands, maybe millions of others. But his genius is to bring together a time, a market, a product, a mesmeric personality and some paint. With me, he scores higher as a HowBoy – the sheer power of how he does things causes the consistent triumph of style over substance.

We should also be grateful for one other lesson. *No cause is lost.* We saw it with Steve Case and the 'cockroach' approach to Dream. We saw resilience with James Dyson. This guy took both to the extreme. Of course, you have to believe, you have to have faith – but if you do, then you must refuse to let it die. Steve Jobs did a standing jump of about 90 feet, from the bottom of watery grave to the top of a pile of amazed competitors, delighted investors, bemused commentators and delirious fans.

Now, if we could only find a guy like that for my soccer team.

NUTTER SCORE:

Dream Merchant: Three stars

HowBoy: Four stars

HERB KELLEHER

12

I AM LOOKING FORWARD TO THIS ONE. For one thing, I do not have many heroes in life generally and in business specifically – but if I did, this guy would figure in both lists. I will also reveal a couple of things about myself – notably the fundamental reason that caused me to leave big business and the fact that I remain, as yet, an undiscovered marketing genius.

Herb Kelleher has run Southwest Airlines in the US for the best part of its thirty-year existence. For those of you – and you will surely be based outside the US – who have never heard of him or the company, at this stage all I will tell you is that Southwest is a 'cut-price' airline.

Now then. I'm ashamed to admit it, but I was passing an idle moment scanning the UK's *Daily Telegraph* newspaper recently. In between the Tory ranting, and the obituaries for guys who magnificently took out a German machine gun post in 1941 and then did nothing for 60 years,[1] I came across an advert. It was also for a 'cut-price' airline, this time European, which trades under the brand name of 'Go'.

I am looking at the advert right now. It is quite big – 17cms by 25cms. I have no idea if it was repeated, either in the same paper on other occasions, or in other papers. Even if it wasn't, it represents a significant media spend. The message was clear: it printed examples of the percentage of flights on time from London to three, named airports in December 2000, and compared Go's results with a direct 'cut-price' competitor, Easyjet. As they are now in the public domain, I list their advertised comparisons:

	Go	Easyjet
From London to:		
Belfast	73%	58%
Edinburgh	72%	42%
Glasgow	72%	51%

Powerful stuff. However, if you assume branding to be the science of *distinction* in cluttered and competitive marketplaces, let's just reflect on what distinction the marketing gurus in Go are communicating to us, the consumers. A communication, by the way, that has cost big money to get to us. Here's the message I get – *Fly 'Go' and we only piss off thirty percent of our customers.* The Americans, separated famously from the Brits only by a common language, have a wonderfully descriptive phrase for this kind of marketing. They call it *Our Product Sucks Less.*

---

[1] In my book, if you take out a German machine gun post, you are entitled to do nothing for the next 60 years. However, if you add up the total of German machine gun posts taken out single-handedly, and which have been recorded in the Telegraph's obituaries, it comes to 1,825, 663,904. Enough already.

I am now about to release my marketing genius. I am going to invent an advert for Herb Kelleher's Southwest Airlines, which is also a Cheapo-Cheapo. How about this:

SOUTHWEST AIRLINES
Fly with US because we have:

- The highest customer service ratings
- The youngest fleet and best safety record
- The fewest cancellations
- The most emulated airline
- The lowest staff turnover
- No staff lay-offs
- The most productive workforce
- Outstanding stock price performance
- Steady growth record
- A conservative balance sheet
- Stability and profitability
- Oh yes, nearly forgot: THE LOWEST FARES[2]

It is a marketing position that does not confirm that cheap is bad. It is a market position that screams that cheap can also be good.

Southwest's wonderful story is essentially built around about Herb Kelleher. There were other seminal figures around at the genesis

---

[2] Yes, yes, I know. I'm blushing – but it's just a natural talent. I am available on a selective basis for major brands that need short, sharp, penetrating marketing campaigns. Minimum personal retainer is about 1 mill (sterling) per month.

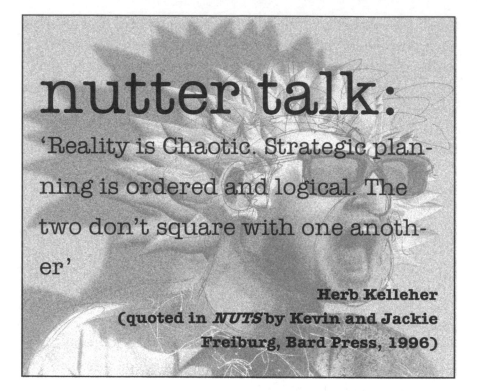

nutter talk:

'Reality is Chaotic. Strategic planning is ordered and logical. The two don't square with one another'

Herb Kelleher
(quoted in *NUTS* by Kevin and Jackie
Freiburg, Bard Press, 1996)

of the airline in the early 1970s, and he is now handing the 'baton' for day-to-day running of the company to two hand-picked successors. It is also the nature of the man to downplay his own role in the company's success – pointing, as is his wont, to a collection of dedicated people who have frequently defied gravity – corporately as well as literally – with him. But you cannot escape the man, even if you wanted to. Which I don't.

Now, here's the bit I love. He seems to have built a spectacular dream by – I need a new font here – **HAVING FUN**.

Yes, that's right. In the modern business world, which is symbolised by stress, greed, fear, pressure, doing wrong things, imbalance, exclusion, skipped lunches, alienation, no-smoking, no-smiling and paranoia, this Wild-Turkey-swilling, tattooed madman has built a dream business while having the time of his life.

This Fun thing – or, rather, the lack of it – is, I believe, more important to the workplace than most people realise. In my case, it represents the dominant reason why I left Big Business a few years ago, determined never to work for anybody else again and to forget one person a day for the rest of my life. Quite simply, I had stopped enjoying business. It was no fun anymore. All those negative factors I listed in the previous paragraph appeared in my life on a regular basis, and after about a quarter-century of serial over-achievement, I thought *bollocks to it.*

The good news, for me, is that I had a choice. The bad news, for you, is that you probably haven't. Tomorrow you must go to some grey building, report to a grey boss and do grey work. Which is why this guy is so important. He is fun, and anything but grey. He is multi-coloured, and succeeded in a tough competitive businesses without compromising his style and attitude. In a world where professionalism is synonymous with a long face, and the word 'silly' has been torn out of all dictionaries, this guy not only survived, he thrived. We need to look deeper. We need – desperately – to see if there is stuff we can beg, borrow or steal from him. If we can, there is hope.

A Charter for Fun in business, that's what we are after. And, like all things that appear simple at first sight, it's not. If you put Kelleher under the microscope, you do see a confident, sure-footed extrovert with a great sense of humour. That's not a great help to us, because we can't easily copy any of them. But a slightly deeper look shows us a shrewd businessman – capable of recognising the benefits of Fun in the workplace, and able to institutionalise, if not his nature, then a bunch of ideas, activities, programmes, policies and procedures that create it. Just reading about these can be entertaining enough – but we can learn from them, and maybe steal some at the same time.

Let me list a bunch that I think I've identified:

I'll start with the obvious one, and get it out of the way: *lead by example.* Even in a big organisation, it is astonishing how the attitude and behaviour of the leader figure gets reflected in the way ordinary folk think and behave. Even if they've never met him or her. Let me give a couple of examples from my life to make the point. When I took over Burger King, as I entered my office for the first time, a stunning looking blonde woman appeared from nowhere and began talking about redesigning my office. It transpired that anytime any executive changed offices, a serious designer (it was she) was called in to 'help' spend the appropriate budget. In my case it was (I'm not making this up) $50,000. I had made a personal rule not to take any decisions for the first week or so, and promptly broke it. I politely got rid of her. I said nothing, but – amazingly – the practice disappeared from my executive team and was never seen again. I did the same thing the first time a stretch limo arrived for me. Amazingly, the practice of taking a limo to the toilet also disappeared. And so on.

It is natural that people watch a leader, and they are influenced. It is not just sycophancy; it is about making life easier. It is about changing the brand of engine oil in your car. What happens is that other people watch the people who have been directly influenced by the leader, and they, in turn, are influenced. You have a leader who hates voice mail? Guess what? Within a week nobody in the organisation is using it. Nothing has to be written down, it just 'happens'.

Kelleher's ability to influence the whole of his business by his behaviour and attitude is legendary – and some of it is instinctive and natural. You can't really go to a college and learn it. But some of it is planned and proactive, and we can learn from that. In March 1992, Southwest had a 'Cease and Desist' case against them for (unwittingly) using a rival's advertising. Kelleher's options were to obey, or fight in court – at least that's how I would have seen them. He found a third option. He booked Dallas stadium, and in front of a full house of manic employees from both companies he *arm-wrestled* the rival chairman for the right to use the slogan. Can you imagine the impact of 'Malice in Dallas' as it became known? Externally, it was like buying media to tell the world what your company is like – it even solicited a smiling note from President Bush. Internally, within

Southwest Airlines, it must have been like taking a legal Ecstasy drug. People get high on this stuff – it's so rare in business.

Kelleher isn't just about 'Malice in Dallas' – he's about a constant, 30-year stream of personal leadership examples of making business fun. His behaviour is pointed outwards at appropriate audiences, and INWARDS at his own team and organisation. His attitude and behaviour, delivered with such consistency and impact, and over such a long period, has permeated to the furthest corners of the smallest office. Just as my people stopped pissing money away on office furniture and limos, Southwest people took the hint and *had fun*.

Second idea – it doesn't – it surely can't – do any harm to *institutionalise the idea of Fun*. The articulated Southwest philosophy has eleven primary attitudes. Here are four of the eleven:

Irreverence is OK

It is OK to be yourself

Have Fun at work

Take competition seriously, but NOT YOURSELF

I've seen corporate 'Mission' and 'Value' statements by the dumpster-load,[3] and – as I have written elsewhere – I have little time for them. Full of Crumbug. In fairness, my survey of the science had not yet come across one in which about a third of the content was pointed at who I saw in the shaving mirror each day, and was telling that person to *lighten up at work*. On it's own, I doubt it can deliver a culture, but mixed with leadership by example, and what follows, it reinforces the idea that Fun is OK. Working hard is also OK, as is being successful. But Fun is too.

Kelleher is clever in harnessing fun to business challenges. At the drop of a hat, he will take some threat on Southwest's radar screen and *turn a challenge into a Cause*. In the early days of the com-

---

[3] Which is where the vast majority belong.

pany, he really had no choice. There were few people in Southwest, and they were fighting for survival as worried competitors fought to keep them grounded. It was relatively easy to get his people, and selected external audiences, to 'rally' around the injustice of it all, and the courtroom dramas gave him fuel aplenty.

There is no doubt that this David – as in Goliath – mentality was formative in shaping the company's culture, but the power and momentum from becoming a Cause cannot have escaped the shrewd Herb. It was meat and drink to his leadership style and the corporate culture he wanted. The modern Southwest, now untouchable by predatory competitors, still uses the concept of a Cause very effectively. It hangs its hat on an array of community causes principally (and I believe this) because it wants to be a good neighbour – but also for the impact that it has inside and outside the company. When United Airlines launched a shuttle service, in direct competition with Southwest, Kelleher's response, with internal rallying cries and external adverts, positioned the company as the last man in a sort of corporate Alamo. That's the Alamo of Texan last-stand fame, not the car rental guys. If you worked for the company, it must have seemed like you were defending democracy itself.

Fun can also come from *controlled naivety*. Let's play the fool, and we can get away with murder. Er … you can get away with more than that, you can get away with reinventing a whole industry. Take, for example, the critical time a commercial aircraft spends at the airport gate – while one lot of passengers de-plane, the thing is cleaned, and then another lot get on board. I am really familiar with the timing, as I have witnessed it with my nose pressed up against airport windows many times. It takes about half an hour, MINIMUM. Not with Southwest, it doesn't. It takes ten minutes – which is a HUGE benefit for a low-price/short-haul carrier. How did they get that performance? Hee Hee! We didn't know any different! *We put people in charge that didn't know it couldn't be done.* What a lark! No boarding cards; flight crews clean up; no food remnants to get rid of, everybody chips in. My, isn't this FUN?

Yup, – it's Fun. It also rewrites existing restrictive practices. Why? How? Well, can you believe people don't mind behaving like that? No, that's wrong – *they actually have FUN behaving like that, if it's carefully and thoughtfully done.* If you take this lesson with you, remember both parts of that last sentence.

We started this book with Benetton using shocking and outrageous images to create impact. Steve Jobs did it with the *1984* advert. You can also create impact with *Outrageous Fun*. Nothing that has impact will please everybody, and you risk the minority being alienated in the cause of the majority loving what you do – and changing their consumer behaviour as a result. Kelleher is a master of outrageous fun. His early cabin crews consisted largely of female Texan cheerleaders, recruited because they had legs right up to the maker's nameplate and who were dressed in company skirts that hid little of them. Today, the idea would be nuked by the Politically Correct Police – then, it hit the media like a brick hits a millpond. When Northwest Airlines – unwisely – claimed to be Number 1 in customer satisfaction, Kelleher's response was to take out advertising space, and announce the following to a delighted public. I can't cut it – here it is in full:

> '*After lengthy deliberation at the highest*
> *levels, and extensive consultation with*
> *our legal department, we have arrived*
> *at an official corporate response to*
> *Northwest Airline's claim to be*
> *Number One in Customer Satisfaction:*
> Liar, Liar. Pants on fire'

I have very few regrets about anything. I am one of the luckiest people on the planet, and jealous of nobody.[4] But I wish, I wish, I WISH I had written and published that, or its equivalent. I had enough

---

[4] This is not strictly true. Under extreme pressure I will admit to being jealous of (in no particular order of priority): a) Denis Law – for being talented and enjoying it; b) Brendan Behan – ditto; and c) whoever's married to Sigourney Weaver.

chances, enough resources and plenty of ammo. When I was leading Burger King, McDonalds put a ton of money behind two product-launches. One was called the McLean, a 'healthy' burger that had *seaweed* in it. The other was called the McRib, and it looked as though it had just been dug up from a World War I battlefield. If only I had taken out some media space and made fun of them, Kelleher style. My life would not have been in vain. The message, from Kelleher to us, to learn, is – if you are going to have fun, occasionally press the 'outrageous' button. You may as well get noticed. It's actually more Fun.

Kelleher is not the first, nor will he be the last, to realise that the right choice of people can deliver many things for a business (and its leader). The Jürgen Schrempps of the world treat their workforces like Kleenex, and – done effectively, ruthlessly and consistently – it can take you a distance. Don't get me started on that.

Others have realised that if you can capture the hearts and minds of your people, you will release an energy that can make a difference to the distinction of your product and service in the market place. Kelleher takes this concept one stage further. He believes that Fun is an integral part of his business alchemy – affecting both the company's internal AND external effectiveness and efficiency. So, what does he do? He hires *Disciples Of Fun*.

In a quarter century and more of business on both sides of the Atlantic, I have been involved, directly and indirectly, in thousands (?) of recruiting and interviewing processes. I have never come across a selection process so geared to hiring Disciples Of Fun as that of Southwest. At the interview or screening stage, you are asked if – how – you have *used* humour in your past work environment. You are invited to cite examples of how you have used humour to defuse a difficult situation. If a company can be this serious about recruiting people with a sense of humour, and they are led by a guy who is a living, consistent example, it stops being rhetoric and starts happening. These folk are serious about Fun. Pause here, and stack this process up against how you choose people, and those you've already got. You could lighten up, you know.

If and when you have these people on board, the job's only half done. Kelleher makes no bones about the work being hard, and that personal productivity levels and flexibilities are above the industry norm. If you bring them in smiling, you've got to *keep them smiling*. Kelleher realised at the outset that you can't just do this by behaving like somebody who has wandered off a Monty Python film set. Sure, that kind of act inspires people, particularly if they have been recruited to have a high propensity to be inspired by mavericks and madmen. But it's not enough on its own. Kelleher is the nearest I have seen to someone treating people who are enjoying themselves as *tangible assets of the business*. So, he *invests in them* as you would to protect the value of the asset. He rewards them for the success their attitude brings – investing 15% of company pre-tax operating income in a profit-sharing plan (of which at least 25% of any such award goes to the purchase of Southwest stock).

In parallel with investing in them, he *champions them*. He openly fights for and defends his employees – from refusing to lay-off staff when times are hard, to standing up for them on the occasions where a Customer From Hell fires in a heat-seeking missile.

He invests in them, he champions them and he *celebrates their successes*. Correction, he celebrates everything. And I mean EVERY-THING. And I also mean he CELEBRATES. Southwest is renowned for partying at the drop of a hat – a small business triumph, an anniversary, somebody recovering from a cold, ten minutes without rain – ANYTHING. It usually involves fancy dress, and guess who will cancel a high-profile industry trip to Washington to attend the impromptu party, usually in the wildest costume? Go on, guess. These folk are happy campers because he keeps 'em smiling. The scary thing is that there's nothing here you couldn't do – to some degree.

There is a final dimension to this Charter for Fun, and it's a really odd one. I am convinced, however, that Southwest's conservative approach to growth was a factor in supporting the critically important internal climate in the company. This is not about being fat, lazy, comfortable and overstaffed – Southwest is famous for being quite the opposite. But it is about being prudent in the company's business growth aspirations. Southwest only took on new routes when it was fully resourced to do so, and they knew they would make money. They never outran their supply lines. *They never drowned their people.* They never exposed their people to impossible stress and pressures from taking on too much new stuff. In the end, their growth proved to be an eye-opener, but they got there in bite-sized chunks. They never lost control, and the lesson is that if you want the hearts and minds of your people, remember it is they who have to digest your growth for you. If they can handle it, all the other stuff can work. If they can't, everything else is a waste of time.

Now, let's flip back and pick out the black bits. It reflects Kelleher's Charter for Fun: *lead by example; institutionalise the idea of fun; make 'causes' out of challenges; use controlled (targeted) naivety; create impact with occasional outrageous fun; hire disciples of fun; keep them smiling and don't drown your people.*

If that charter bears any resemblance to your workplace, you are in a unique company. You are also working with unique company. The odds are heavily against either.

But why? Why does it *have to be so?* And could you change or influence your deal? How hard would it be for you to take bits of all of the Charter points, or all of some of them, and to try to lighten your place up? Sure, Kelleher backed this charter up with a shrewd business mind, but he achieved profound success. But what he proved, surely beyond reasonable doubt, is that success doesn't have to be *instead of* fun. You can have success *as well as* having the time of your life. Oh, happy, happy day.

Southwest is now facing the future without Herb Kelleher. A new CEO is in place, along with a new president – both from inside the company, both veterans and both steeped in the corporate culture. Kelleher will remain chairman for three years. I guess the jury is out as to whether this iconic man, rated by many as the best corporate leader in America today, will leave an unfillable hole, and that the glorious Southwest Airlines story will prove to be one of rising on the back of his unique talents and then falling off when he leaves.

I don't think so. Corporate cultures are not what is written down in fancy annual reports and framed on the corporate cafeteria walls. Corporate culture is not something that is an 'end' result, coming from a bunch of policies and procedures dreamed up by HR. It evolves, it is not implemented. Corporate culture is something that exists. It is the air that a company breathes, and it governs the health and life forms of the business.

Kelleher's greatest legacy is that he has orchestrated a genuine, robust, tangible corporate culture that now doesn't need him. Why? Because it is enjoyable, satisfying and successful. It is in the interests of the Southwest people to keep it that way, because the alternative is what the rest of us have. It is, therefore, more self-sustaining than the norm, thanks to the genius of this latter day Crazy Horse. My belief is that you couldn't kill it, in the short term, if you tried. The new folk on the bridge are not strangers to any dimension of it, and neither is anybody else in Southwest.

This Dream was built on Fun, by a master HowBoy. And it was built so well, with the foundations laid so solidly, that I believe there will be much to come.

NUTTER SCORE:

Dream Merchant: Four stars

HowBoy: Off the scale

HOWARD SCHULTZ

I F YOU STUDY THE HABITS of retail service customers, you will be interested in a pattern of behaviour exhibited by my wife and I recently. For a couple of years, if both of us were home at our house in Miami, our morning ritual was to walk our golden retriever early before it got too hot. We would then jump in the soft-top and drive to a local coffee shop to arm ourselves with an appropriate dose of caffeine so that we could face the rigours of another day in paradise.

Responding to a set of domestic circumstances that would take another book to cover, we suddenly found ourselves, complete with retriever, in another house, a few miles away, in the infamous Coconut Grove. The first morning, we set off and found a new dog-walk. When that was finished, without saying a word to each other, we got in the car and drove past about five coffee shops, and went back to our regular one. As it happens it was (and still is) a Starbucks. The one right opposite the University of Miami on South Dixie Highway.

To this day I am not fully sure why we did that – and, what is more, continued to do that. You see, one of the coffee shops we drove past on our way back to our old favourite was another Starbucks.

Whatever our reasons for this strange behaviour, they are at the core of the mystery that goes by the name of retailing. Just how do you shape your total offering so that customers are attracted to you more often than they are attracted to your competitors? How do you do that so that sometimes these customers will do that to the point of irrationality?

What our behaviour illustrated, of course, was that – in the space of a dozen years – the Starbucks brand had become one of the most powerful consumer magnets in the world. From a standing start. It also illustrates, to me at least, that Starbucks – like most retail brands – is about more than just a product. And, while we are at it, it also illustrates to me that they are about more than just 'location, location, location'.

I had watched the Howard Schultz and the Starbucks phenomenon unfold with more than just passing interest. Hell, I was in the same general industry and, given that he didn't get his plane into the air until the late 1980s, I was operating in most of the same markets at largely the same time. I said I paid it more than a passing interest. It transpires, for a number of reasons, that I didn't pay it enough.

I left Big Business, of my own choice, in the mid 1990s – loosely explaining (mostly to myself) this strange move by muttering that I had stopped 'enjoying' it. Indeed, those are the terms I have used elsewhere in this book. If anybody asked me *why* I wasn't enjoying it, I just shrugged and looked vacant. I didn't feel I had to explain anything further. I would mumble something about stopping laughing, and/or wanting to do something different and/or wanting more time with the family and/or I was pissed off with airplanes and yada yada yada. It was not until a few years later that it occurred to me that I had quit because there was an increasing element of failure in my career.

That kinda hurts to write down even now. If my wonderful dad is perched on his cloud looking down on me typing this, he will be in danger of falling off if he can read it. He will not understand. He saw me 'rise' from teenage fuckwit to become chairman and CEO of one of the world's great brands in just over twenty years. His only begotten son, who kept him awake at nights, became somebody whose accomplishments gave him great pride. And it is true that I have 'accomplished' more than I could have ever dreamed – if you measure that conventionally. I have more money than I need, and have walked away from ten times more again. Great family, lovely house, nice lifestyle. I have held corporate office at vertigo-inducing levels, and had my face on the front of *Fortune* magazine.

At this point my editor is thinking of writing something in the margin. He's going to say: 'Excuse me Barry, but isn't this bit supposed to be about Howard Schultz's success? We seem to have drifted into you and your boring failure. Readers haven't paid for that. Is it possible that we could, say, sometime today, get this back on track?' Absolutely. Read this next bit (you cranky bastard).

After leaving Big Business, I was still in the US, and still acc-en-tu-ating the positives about why I had left it. I was invited (er … paid) to give a speech to a business convention somewhere. I knew I was one of two or three speakers, and I also knew that I had a tight set of logistics to handle at the end of my speech to get to my plane to get me back home. I finished my speech to the usual rapturous applause and, pausing only to pick up some of the *lingerie* that had been thrown on the stage during all the excitement, disappeared backstage, already unhooking my microphone. Inadvertently, I bumped into the next speaker – a tall, classy looking guy, with a deceptively firm handshake and quiet, thoughtful, tone of voice. He said some very nice things about my speech, and then went on stage, as the sound system announced his name: Howard Schultz.

I had no intention of staying but, to get out of the auditorium, I had to walk up the side passageway by the seats. As I was doing that, I saw him leave the 'safety' of his spot behind the speaker's lectern, meander to the centre of the stage and start to talk. Within a minute, to my own annoyance and not inconsiderable inconvenience, I was hooked.

I can't give you the contents in detail. I shouldn't try, because content is only part of a speech – as the demented Eddie Izzard says, impression is about seventy percent how you look, twenty percent how you sound and only ten percent about what you say. In summary, however, let me just say that he made some simple points about the difference between professional (NBA), and amateur (college), basketball in the USA. To the detriment of the former, I might add. Despite the NBA being technically better, and involving zillions more dollars, it did not have the integrity and values of the 'real' thing. He then linked this to the Starbucks story and told the audience, without any embarrassment or blushing, how he had attempted to build a mighty brand on integrity and values. He stated, simply, that the dream of the brand was only partly about coffee. It was actually much more about making the celebration of human spirit the foundation on which everything in Starbucks was founded. I can't do him justice here, so catch him on one of these speeches if you can. For me, the effect was like an epiphany. About three years after it ended, I realised my career had been tinged with failure.

Bear with me here. This is not about me, it is about him – but to make his success come alive for you, in a way *you can then use* – I need to use myself as a comparison. You see, I had a huge brand in the palm of my hand. It was actually bigger than Starbucks. Sure, I didn't own it – but then again, Schultz didn't and doesn't own Starbucks. In my defence, I did not have the chance to shape and affect the culture of Burger King *from its genesis* in the way that Schultz was able to do with Starbucks. That is quite a big factor as it is far more difficult to change this sort of stuff than to create it – but that can only be listed as a partially mitigating circumstance.

Here's what happened to the pair of us around the end of the 1980s. We faced three enemies at our respective business gates. You may recognise them as the same ones camping outside yours. With hindsight – and with frightening clarity – I can now see my failings. You see, *I let them in, he kept them out.*

Was it important? Remember, I got all the medals and money. Yes it was. I had a dream, but lost it because of these three enemies. I can count my money all day, but it doesn't compensate. I will never be in a book like this – so digest the next bit closely if you want your dream to happen, at whatever level.

I will dig into these three Dream-enemies, one by one.

The first is *short-termism*, the bane of free market capitalism. The philosophy of GrandMet, who owned Burger King, and who were my employers, was simple. If you delivered the short-term earnings per share goals every year for twenty years, hey presto, you would deliver the long-term goals. So, you did whatever was needed, in any particular year, to deliver the figures. I repeat – whatever was needed. Which I did, including some stupid things that made no sense at all – viewed, frankly – from any stakeholder's angle.

This whole subject is given added complexity if you are a competing subsidiary or division in a larger corporation. In these cases, you sometimes have to do even more stupid things to your part of the business to bail out another part that is struggling. I did that too. I cannot remember *one* occasion when I didn't achieve – or over-achieve – my subsidiary's contribution to the parent's EPS goals. On a number of occasions, however, I achieved it by eroding brand equity, selling the family silver to pay the butler, ignoring medium-term opportunities and alienating crucial groups of people – franchisees, employees and vendors. Sometimes I did all of the above – they are far from mutually exclusive.

Are short-term earnings per share important? Of course they bloody well are. There is simply no point in investing unless you can get a better return on your money than would be the case from leaving it on deposit somewhere. Free market Darwinism ensures the best projects get the resources they need and the success they deserve. But earnings per share are not the be-all and end-all of capitalism. *They should not mask, or be masked by, crass business decisions.*

Let's turn the clock back to the late 1980s. Schultz had facilitated the acquisition and control of Starbucks – at that time a small, Seattle-based company that wasn't sure about the whole espresso-retailing thing. It was still a private company, and would remain so through four, private-funding placements until the company finally offered shares to the public in 1992. Anybody who has been near this territory will tell you that investors, at this stage of a start-up, come in many shapes and sizes but usually have one thing in common. They want high returns, and they want them early – because they see themselves taking high risks with a start-up. We are not talking about patient capitalists here.

Schultz quite deliberately adopted policies that would sub-optimise the short-term earnings per share of Starbucks. On the earnings side of the equation, he insisted that all the company's employees, including *baristas*, had private, health-care insurance cover – an expensive corporate overhead. Not only that, all concerned knew that it was a commitment that couldn't be rolled back, and one that would get hugely more expensive. On the shares side of the equation, he insisted that the investing shareholders diluted their stakes by offering share options to all employees – again down to the front ranks. In summary, therefore, these two policies guaranteed less earnings, on the one hand, and more issued shares on the other. The short-term earnings per share performance of the company was, therefore, deliberately flattened – in order to invest in attracting and retaining the right people. In 1987, Starbucks had 17 stores. As I write this, less than 15 years later, they have 4500. It seems to have worked. Investor returns have reflected that growth.

Now, let me ask a question – maybe of myself. What do I think the shareholders would rather have had, given hindsight? A short-term 30% return on equity, or the thousands of percent return that came with the healthy growth of a genuinely adding-value brand? Exactly.

The second enemy he had at his gate, as I did (and you probably do), is the enemy I call *'accounting for people'*. We have all grown to accept the way we handle hiring and paying people from a financial accounting standpoint, but if you landed from Mars and looked at it you would see it for what it is – the biggest load of bollocks in the universe.

Here's how I think they do it on Mars. They figure out that, if you are running a business where people sell coffee to other people, you will need to invest in some buildings and some people. So you go and buy a building and you buy a person, both for an appropriate sum of money. They both go on the balance sheet, not the profit and loss account. Because Martian GAAP is very sophisticated, however, you then depreciate these assets over a period of time, which is an operating cost – but if they grow in value, either intrinsically or be-cause you have invested to improve them, you can reflect that on your balance sheet and operating statement. Should anybody want to value you business – hey presto – they would recognise that your buildings and people added shareholder value, and would both, therefore, be on the balance sheet.

Here on earth, we do it slightly differently. We don't buy peo-ple's working time as an asset, we rent it as an expense. People are not strengths of the business, reflected on its balance sheet; they are weaknesses, jacking up its costs. At all times, it is in the accounting and earnings-per-share interests of the business to have the mini-mum number of people on the books at the lowest possible cost. There is simply no accounting provision for the benefits accruing to the business from the efforts of (say) a stable, well-compensated and highly-effective sales person – as compared to the downside associ-ated with a flow of cheap itinerant labour flowing through that job position. Or, worse still, nobody in that job at all.

Again, it would be stupid to advocate that labour costs are just really a nice-to-know statistic as you pursue your corporate dream.

They are critically important, but costs that are way too low can be as bad for business effectiveness and efficiency just as much as those that are way too high.

Of course, anybody running a service-based retail operation will tell you that variable labour costs are the single biggest item on the operating statement – usually bigger than the cost of product and/or real estate involved. If you get them out of whack, you bring the whole house down – so you must control them. All that is correct, but so is having the *right level* of people in place to support your brand, at all levels. So, if your brand relies on people to provide its winning distinction in the market place, then you have to fly in the face of the accountants and resource for them, even if it means paying for assets on the expense sheet.

Here, again, Schultz stood his ground. In his eyes Starbucks was never just about coffee. A Starbucks coffee shop offered the world a Third Place, somewhere other than the office or the home, to hang out, relax and socialise. Starbucks' people added real value to the brand – from the mystery of the *barista*'s operations to the general conviviality of the place. So he treated them as assets. He took pains to find the right ones, and then took pains to keep them. Some of that took money (providing better-than-average wages, health care etc.), and some of it took attitude (giving them stock options, investing in their training and development, listening and responding to them etc.). Whatever it took, he did it. If it needed money, he found it from elsewhere or did without. He knew that if he treated his people like assets, there was a chance they would perform like assets – and that if that happened, the returns would come. One day. In Bucketfuls.

How did I stack up? We can get fancy and/or detailed, and I can plead I did better than a whole host of my peers. But if we peel it all back to the core, and ask the savage question: *Were the 280,000 people in Burger King an asset, or an expense, of the business in my eyes?* My answer would be that, apart from a handful of my Centurions, I saw them as an expense. I *dreamed* that they *could* be an asset, even to the level of inventing a TV campaign: *'Burger King – there are 280,000*

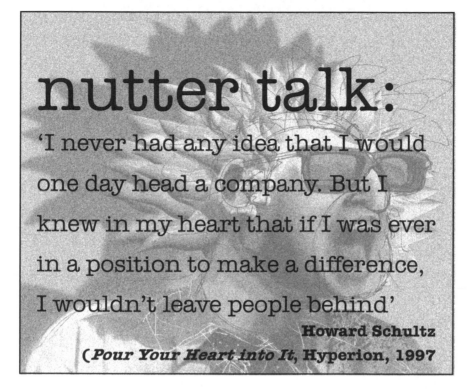

nutter talk:

'I never had any idea that I would one day head a company. But I knew in my heart that if I was ever in a position to make a difference, I wouldn't leave people behind'

Howard Schultz
(*Pour Your Heart into It*, Hyperion, 1997

of us and everyone gives a shit.' But that's all it was, a dream. From my start position, I had no idea how to reach out and nurture all those people, most of whom were employed by franchisees in any event. I had a picture, but saw no way that I could completely restructure the paradigms and culture involved – without taking ten years and charging $20 for a Whopper Hamburger. So, apart from dancing around the edges and whacking in some token stuff, people in the Burger King system – that is, the important people, the ones who deal face-to-face with the customers day in day out – stayed as expenses. People in Starbucks are assets. It's a different mental accounting, but the results are tangible. Score a success for Howard, a failure for me. You choose for yourself.

Schultz had a third enemy at the gate – which I'm going to call *the temptation of superficial brand equity*. Again, he refused to let this enemy in, I didn't. You might have the choice.

The essence of this enemy is that it is (relatively) easy, if you are a brand owner, to buy consumer trial of your product or service. It is, however, extremely difficult to buy their loyalty. In fact, I am not sure you can buy it – all you can buy is another trial. Loyalty to a brand is that wonderful state where customers start to act irrationally to get hold of their favourite product – even when barriers have been put in the way. The kind of consumer behaviour that forced the abandonment of New Coke, and sees folk like me and my wife driving past one Starbucks to get to another.

Brand managers will recite the brand cycle like a mantra – first you create awareness, then you generate a trial purchase, then you seek loyalty – which enables you to shoot for higher purchase frequency and/or higher spend per visit. There's nothing much wrong with that – it is the assumptions on how you get it that start the wheels falling off.

Most brand managers will tell you that advertising spend, measured in currency, is the key to all those stages. They will add that, without copious amounts of bought media, and a hugely expensive creative agency, you haven't a chance with a modern brand in today's markets. That was fine when there were but a few choices of available products and services, and limited media – but modern life has seen an explosion in market competition and media to the degree that consumers are nearly blind and deaf to the thousands of entreating brand messages that pop up in front of them every day. Quite frankly, I doubt if God would have a big enough media budget to launch his brand name, and secure extensive loyalty, if he started today and used any of the brand mangers I have known. With the possible exception, that is, of Howard Schultz.

There is one particularly fascinating fact buried in the tons of positive data you can glean from ten minutes exploring Starbucks on the Web. From 1987–97, the first ten years of the life of the Schultz-controlled Starbucks, *the company spent more on employee training than it did on advertising.* Clearly, something (or somebody) else generated the awareness that generated more consumer trial (etc. etc.). As Holmes said to Watson, when everything else has been deemed impossible, whatever's left, however unlikely, holds the key to the answer. The 'somebody else' was the customer base itself – telling other potential customers about this brand. While they were doing that, they were also showing remarkable brand loyalty and purchase frequency themselves. Schultz built the brand, one customer at a time. He illustrated the business equivalent of 'trickle-down economics' – one customer tells three others, each of whom tell three others (that's nine) each of whom tells another three. That's the maths that takes you from 17 stores to 4500 in a decade and a half.

Let's make, and record, a deduction – that the spend on training did the job that advertising would have done. Hell, no – the spend on training did MORE than any spend on advertising would have done.

Here's where Schultz showed that talent that Kelleher, Disney and a bunch of the others in this book have shown. He understood what the *real demand* was out there, and supplied a product for it. It's only when you hit THAT bull's-eye that you get a consumer response that *sees them do your marketing for you*. Coffee, and the integrity of the beans and roasting are important to Starbucks, but the brand is not just about packaged or espresso coffee. By luck or judgement, and it might have been the former at first, and the latter in the 1990s, Schultz provided a product that met two of the most powerful market demands of our time – neither of which has to do with coffee.

The first is the Celebration of the Small Self-Indulgency – a strange but growing behavioural trait in modern consumers. It is a response to the hassle and horse-shit of today's pressured existence, and it manifests itself in an unassailable need to reward yourself with something small and *relatively* expensive – but cheap in the scheme of things. You can't afford a holiday in Hawaii, but it's been a shitty day so you are going to buy yourself a Häagen-Dazs ice cream. It actually costs a lot of money for what it is, compared to the competitors – but it's still only a couple of pounds or dollars. And that's part of the fun. Substitute Starbucks for the ice cream brand, and there you go.

The second powerful demand trend is the reawakened need for the Third Place. Ironically, coffee houses provided for this need in the past, but faded away as the domestic home became the social entertainment centre and work and commuting took up more of the day. The pubs and diners filled in the gaps. Then, guess what? You don't know what you've got till it's gone, and, as the world shrunk, Europe's still-existent café society looked a hell of a good idea again. Schultz opened a few, and the lid blew off.

From the get-go, he knew this wasn't just about coffee. He knew it would be about people. Hence the training, the Bean Stock,[1] the people being treated as assets, the listening and responding, and the health insurance. This is not *instead* of having a great coffee product, it is *as well as* that.

I think he knew from very early on that Starbucks could be a massive winner – but only if he really understood the epicentre of the true demand, and consistently delivered a product that met it. Most retail service brand managers, given that opportunity, would insist that their success would be built around 'product, product, product' or 'location, location, location'. The genius of this guy is that he knew it would come from '*People, people, people – albeit with a great product and great locations as well*'. Once he realised that, he never wavered. As the three enemies to building a brand this way attacked his gates, he held out.

This guy fought off short-termism, the anally-retentive accounting principles that insist your winning people cannot be accounted as assets, and the temptation to buy superficial brand equity with money. From my experience, these are some of the most powerful enemies you can have in building a Dream of stature and sustainability. I let too many of them into my fortress, too often.

---

[1] This is the name given to the share option scheme given to all employees. The idea is that it would grow like a bean-stalk (Bean-stock) – geddit? No, I didn't either.

They will come and attack you too, so you must first make up your mind what you want to do when they appear. Then, when you hear the first guns, it's in your hands.

Now then. I have a confession to make. You remember all that stuff about me failing? It was baloney. I was actually smiling when you took it all in. I mean, as if I could have failed. The truth is – I wasn't that bad, and Schultz wasn't that good. The wonderfully named Barney Barnato, the South African mining magnate, once famously addressed a meeting of shareholders: *'Gentlemen'* he announced *'those are my principles. And if you don't like them, I have others'*. You see, Howard wasn't against going against some of his own deeply held beliefs if it suddenly suited him – witness the introduction of skimmed milk, bottled Frappucino and licensed operators into Starbucks against his earlier deep opposition. Conversely, I held out (occasionally) for a few things that Howard would have been proud of. The key to this particular Dream is not about coffee, or locations – or even about people. It is about *choices*, and that is what you can steal from this guy.

Business today, at whatever level, offers choices. They can range from long-term strategic choices to short-term tactical ones. When you look at your project, there will be some principles that, by your definition, and – if necessary – your definition only, *cannot be defiled* if it is to succeed on your terms. There will be others that look like hills that are not worth dying on. Too often, I cheerfully admit, I was like Barney Barnato – if the circumstances didn't suit my principles, I changed the latter. Too often I tried to buy brand equity with a promotion, too often I would cut adding-value people costs if revenues fell short, and too often I succeeded on the day at the expense of the morrow.

I didn't fail, I don't lose sleep, and I have few regrets. *But I didn't build a Dream*. This guy built a major-league Dream by holding firm to some beliefs, and taking the *hard* choices that supported them. That's what you must take away.

Ironically, by building a magnificent Dream in this way, Howard Schultz qualifies, *de facto*, as a Blue-Ribboned HowBoy.

NUTTER RATING:

Dream Merchant: Five stars

HowBoy: Five stars

CONCLUSION:
CAN IT WORK FOR YOU?

14

A T THE OUTSET, I STATED the objectives of the book were to learn a bit, laugh a bit and steal a lot. It's time to concentrate on the third.

All the folk in this book 'made it'. For some, the journey was easier than it was for others. The sheer size of some of their successes enable them to exist in a different league than others. Ironically, some got there in spite of themselves, but they all got there. They also have another thing in common – they all started on low rungs of the ladder, with little but their talent in the way of resources. Indeed, some took that lowly starting point, and worsened it before their great triumphs came.

Nobody reading this book is likely to build a Disneyland or father an Internet Service Provider that leaps to 30 million members from a standing start, against predatory competition, within a decade, because, well, er, it's been done. But there will be new Dream Merchants and HowBoys. Right now, these unknown folk are marshalling their talents and meagre resources, and looking thoughtfully at the overwhelming odds against them. In ten or twenty years' time, if somebody were to repeat this thesis, it will be full of names that neither you nor I have heard of.

I have deliberately biased the contents of this book towards 'recent' Dream Merchants and HowBoys – leaving out the great industrialists of a century ago and more. That was primarily done with this chapter in mind, and there were two clear reasons behind it. First, if we are to learn and steal from these people, it made sense to make the examples as relevant as possible to the circumstances we face. Most of these people worked against a background that is familiar to all of us – i.e. modern markets, institutions, regulations, technology, employment practices and so on. It is no good us trying to ape guys like J.P. Morgan who built a Dream that would be blown out of the water today by anti-trust regulations. These folk journeyed through a territory we know.

The second reason for leaning towards the end of the twentieth century is, I hope, an inspiring one. Not only can these triumphs happen, they can happen to 'ordinary' folk. They can also be huge in size and happen with mind-boggling speed. A good proportion of these triumphs secured their real breakthroughs, momentum and rewards in a decade or so. Just prior to that, not one of these folk would stand out in a crowd that included the likes of you or me splashing about in the shallow end of our business lives.

The first conclusion we draw, which is something of a disappointment to me,[1] is that there is no silver bullet. There is no One Thing that they all did which was the key to success. There isn't even

---

[1] I had hoped, Oh, how I had hoped, that I could whistle through a couple of rapid and obvious conclusions and whack this off to the publishers. However much you love writing and the subject matter, show me an author who isn't pissed off with a book when he gets to the end and I'll show you a liar.

a single Golden Rule that is common to all. Some elements are more evident and appear more often than others, but the striking thing is that is there is a whole range of things that these folk brought to bear, *which you might be able to do,* to some degree.

Let me list them for you. Unfortunately, for both of us, I've identified ten. I've just re-read them, and if you go at my speed it will take you about 17 minutes to get through the section – but if there are a few ideas here that you can steal, and that will turn the project that you are currently contemplating into a winner, then it might be time well spent. I'll pause a minute while you go and get one of those yellow highlighter thingies.

OK? Where was it? Well, I never.

Right, off we go, and I'm going to start with a really obtuse one, so I can get it over with.

1 *Milk your influences.* You are a rare person if you do not have any role models or 'celebrity' influences in your life. In the cases of most people, they are from show business or sport – but it may be a politician, a religious leader, an author or a business icon. On the other hand, it might be an unsung hero or heroine, somebody who quietly makes the world a better place – a teacher, nurse or missionary. You might just have one of the above, or one in each category.

My observation is that these folk have a deeper influence on many folk than they either admit to or (maybe) recognise. They can also help you to succeed in your own challenges, but not without a bit of thought and analysis on your part.

I will work on the basis that the folk who influence you do so positively, and that there are aspects of their way of doing things, and their success, that impress you. Now, I take it further: if you could somehow transfer those positives to the way you go about things, and the project you have right in front of you, then your journey might be easier. Fine, but here's the rub.

This can only work if you can get under the surface, and understand *why* you are so receptive to what they have done.

I'll give an example from my own life. In the mid 1960s I loved Bob Dylan. I have used some of the way he influenced me in business – positively. What I didn't use was his ability to articulate verse, link it with a powerful melody and sing through his nose – because none of that is much use in selling fucking oil, beer and hamburgers, which have been my sequential chosen causes. What I did with my Dylan influence is look underneath the surface, and I found that what really impressed me was *his ability to reinvent himself.* It was not only an ability to reinvent himself, but to do so BEFORE the rest of the world saw the need – while he was still successful in his previous incarnation. Now, that's what I stole, and that is a relevant as anything you will get from a business school.

List the people who you look up to. Then peel them back a bit – why do they appear so positive to you? What is the root – not the surface – cause of their influence on you? Given that you will have a higher propensity to ape these folk than some night-school lecturer or business guru, try and understand their success – and then steal that. Now, go back and scan the chapter on James Dyson. It was from his early influences, and his deeper understanding of what was behind their success, that he learned the power of *combining* technology and design. It worked for him.

2   *Fuse different elements together.* There is a tendency in all of us to seek solutions in and amongst what is familiar to us. It is natural. It represents territory where we are (relatively) knowledgeable and comfortable – and where we feel that if we keep digging we will find our answers. Not one – I repeat, not *one* – of the Dream Merchants and HowBoys in this book triumphed with this one-dimensional approach, and that itself is a lesson.

In a few of the examples, a kind of jigsaw was pieced together – where several pieces all combined to make a unique and powerful whole. I don't think you can rely on the luck and/or judgement involved in that set of circumstances coming over the hill to rescue you. But what you can do is mandate to yourself that your project must have at least one foreign element. And a good way to find the right one is to shoplift.

Again, I give you an example from my own life to illustrate the principle. When I ran an area of retail operations, with a small gaggle of operations folk reporting to me, we used to have our area meetings in a retail outlet – *any one but one of our own.* An open-agenda item was for us to digest our surroundings while we were talking about our business, and then we wouldn't close the meeting until we had identified an idea we could use back in our business. It is amazing how the ideas from a successful drycleaners can transfer to a pub.

There is a mental block to break through here. Houdini, the American escapologist, was beaten only once. In a series of increasingly difficult public escapes early in the twentieth century, he found himself chained to a chair inside a jail cell in a small mid-western US town. Outside the door, the public and the press waited – he had estimated it would take him about twenty minutes to get through all the locks and chains and make his triumphant appearance. This time he never did, and it wasn't until the crowd and press had long gone that they twigged what had knackered him – the jailer had *forgotten to lock the cell door.* All he had to do was walk up to it and turn the handle – but that was not what was familiar to him, so he never thought to try it. Almost every business, and every businessperson, I have come across has a 'door' that they assume is 'locked'. A good place to start looking for a different dimension for your project is to walk up to it and try it. Michael Dell decided to deal *directly* with his own customers, Anita Roddick put her creams and lotions in returnable containers and James Dyson stole the dual cyclone idea from a sawmill. Find a different dimension, and *fuse* it on to what you know. Your project suddenly looks different.

3   *Take a restless pill.* Look, if you are a lazy bugger, there's not much you or I can do about it. Frankly, it doesn't help your cause to be a legendary Dream Merchant or HowBoy if you can't get out of bed, or even if you are one of these annoying folk who seem indolent but are somehow prodigiously productive. This is an area where the optical signals you give off are important.

All is not lost, however. The idea that you have to be a 24/7 workaholic to be successful has been blown out of the water by George Dubya. As I write, he is employed as the president of the most powerful (and complex) country on earth, and he appears to put in about a twenty hours a week. In business, Gerry Robinson, an old GrandMet colleague of mine, who went on to stardom as chairman of Granada, and who would have been in this book had I covered another five names, is famous for not letting his working week interfere too much with the weekend on either side of it. It can be done.

The key is to be restless. It is not just a physical thing, it is a *condition* which has some physical implications. Its component parts are curiosity, momentum, energy and an ability, at times, to be a fourteen carat pain in the arse. There are bees in your bonnet and ants in your pants constantly. You can't leave an idea alone. If somebody says something can't be done, that signals a *start* position in your mind, not an end point. I've been in and around the food and beverage business for longer than I care to remember – and my wife now knows that if we go in a new bar or restaurant the first ten minutes are a dead loss for me as company. I'm working out where the staff are stealing (my ingoing position is that they all do), or what the food margins are. Rather indelicately, I have a dozen books by the lavatory – I hate missing the opportunity to come across an idea I can use in an article or business. A jog or a bike ride is a chance for me to figure a way around some distant, unrelated challenge.

It would seem that Schrempp would be the prime example of this – with his non-stop twitching, smoking, running, jumping, barking, no-sleep approach to life. But if you look a wee bit more deeply at Roberto Goizueta, you'll find more of what I'm trying to articulate and, more importantly, of what you can use. He was not a frenetic man, but he was certainly a restless man. His physical pacing was measured and his style calm – but beneath that, his mind had an energy and momentum that never left the 'cause' alone. Look, too at Anita Roddick – more physical, certainly, but eternally restless in the cause.

4 *Control what you must.* In almost any business project, facing anybody, at any level, there are levers that can be pulled by the person in charge, and other levers that need permission from somebody else. There is stuff you can do yourself, without reference to anybody else, and there is stuff that other people must do for you. It is a modern business maxim that, in the pursuit of optimising shareholder value, you should concentrate on your core competence, and 'outsource' everything else to people who are good at whatever that is. Breweries should not own pubs, for example, and retailers should stay out of financial services. All good common sense, but if anything, the emphasis has all been focused on the outsourcing, with companies proudly getting out of everything from product distribution to the provision of cafeterias, and then taking a bow at the annual shareholders meeting.

For many of the examples in this book, however, the focus remains on the other side of the coin – on what you keep. Or, rather, on what you control. If you sit, pause and look at the challenge facing you, it is likely there are multiple tasks involved in getting to the end point. If you rank them by *leverage* – in other words those tasks that have the most impact on getting the project done on time, on budget and on specification are ranked highest – you will probably find that two or three are what the fancy gurus call *mission critical*. This, for those who can't handle crap like that, is defined by me as: *factors that can't, under any circumstances, be fucked up if the thing is going to succeed.* Now, the emphasis switches. You can't let these babies out of your hands. What's the difference between Michael Dell and most of the other PC manufacturers? He realised that the existing retail distribution chain was failing both the manufacturer and the customer – and that, far from being clever, it was *dumb* for Dell not to own and control its distribution channels. Ditto, Luciano Benetton.

You don't actually have to own it to control it – as Coca-Cola proved by acquiring 49% of their key bottlers. The key word is *control*. This is way beyond the ability to just influence something, it means that you are actually pulling the levers. There may only be a couple of such factors in whatever it is you are facing, but you need to do whatever is necessary to get them in your hands – trading off and outsourcing a whole bundle of non-critical stuff if necessary

5   *Do not masturbate.* Sorry about the sub-title, but I know exactly what I mean and it is one of the most important things we can steal from these folk.

I'll start this with a question, working on the assumption you have all heard of Parker Pens. OK, now – what is the primary market they are in? The fountain-pen market? No, that's not their primary market. The writing instrument market? No, ditto. The communication market? No, ditto again. In my observation, their primary market is the corporate gift market, and their key competition is not from other pens, or other communication devices, but from food hampers and boxes of wine.

It was Albert Einstein who rather startled the world with his thesis that, if you can conceive of something, it can be created. That is a great driving factor for many people in business, who work in an area of speciality – to explore just how far you can go with an existing concept. Just how many billion transistors is it possible to get on a microchip? In short – the challenge is to do it because it can be done. It is the corporate equivalent of playing with yourself, hence the subtitle

Almost without exception, the folk listed in the book paid *no attention* to this as a motivator. The fact that something was actually doable was secondary to the fact that it was wanted or needed. They could see ahead – sometimes around corners – and their vision was all centred around demand. That is, the real demand and the fundamental demand trends.

Disney did not build Disneyland because it could be done, or because he loved plastic castles. He built it because he foresaw the explosive growth in travel and tourism. That was the demand, and he supplied the product. In the early 1970s, America had two categories of population – those who could afford to fly (a tiny, tiny minority) and those who couldn't (the rest). Herb Kelleher was not interested in how fancy and technically excellent the science of flying could be, he saw a huge future demand in enfranchising the rest with the wherewithal to fly. Steve Case didn't use technology to impress people with how technical AOL could be if it wanted, he used technology only to make his service user-friendly and do what the customer wanted. Schultz saw the need for the Third Place, and the need to celebrate the small self-indulgency. Breeze back through the book and open it anywhere – and I guarantee you will not be far away from an example from one of these folk structuring a product or service, or a way of doing business, to satisfy a powerful demand factor.

I have talked in the book how Dream Merchants see future shapes that you and I don't – and that they are usually simple enough in concept terms to be crayoned. Let me take that one stage further – these shapes are usually about a future demand trend. The message to you, for your project, is crystal clear: don't play with yourself. Pleasing yourself is irrelevant. How good you are is also irrelevant if that skill is not used in developing something for which there is a substantial and sustainable need. No more, and no less. Just that.

6   *Pick your challenge.* Not always easy. You must have heard the story of the two shoe salesmen who were sent to India from England earlier this century. Their job was to develop the international market for their products. They went to adjacent, but similar, provinces. Within a week, the first one had wired back to headquarters: *'Nobody wears shoes – no market here – I might as well return home'.* On the same day (amazing coincidence) the second salesman also wired his first report: *'Nobody wears shoes – amazing opportunity – send more staff and stock'.*

    Whether you are one of these enthusiasts who see an opportunity in every challenge, or a pessimist who just sees problem after problem, you can be sure that you will both have an adequate supply of difficulties in modern business. When you are thinking through the future of your project, you will probably be able to identify some future bottlenecks and/or challenges well in advance. Some, of course, will be unpredictable, and you will have to react when they appear – but some are predictable, and you can therefore deal with them proactively. It is unlikely you will be able to avoid them, so the trick is to manage them, and minimise the risk.

    For somebody like Branson, facing external markets, he brings a simple rule into play – attack the market Fat Cats. Whereas most people would shy away from big-name competition, he goes for them – backed by the logic that they actually provide the easier opposition. Their very success has seen them become bloated, sluggish, and slow to respond – and they usually work in markets with high margins, principally because they have made it so. Fertile ground for Virgin, *n'est-ce pas?*

    Look at your barriers to success as far ahead as you can. Is there some way you can manoeuvre to find a smaller, less effective barrier at that stage? If you can see the battle ahead, is there some way you can manage the circumstances so that it is played out on terrain that is to your advantage? Can you *create* diversions, pressures or confusions that make the barrier less intimidating?

This is not just a tactic to be applied externally. Most projects have internal challenges, down to the basics of having key individuals on your side or against. Not many of us have the mentality to kill opponents and then eat them like Schrempp, but we do have some ability to recruit internal champions and neutralise potential internal opponents – provided we think it through clearly, and do what we have to in a timely fashion. Time spent, in advance, on this can prove to be a very effective lubricant for the process.

7   *Wrap your riddle in a mystery and then in an enigma.* This was Churchill's famous description of Russia, borne partly of frustration and partly of admiration. That's not a bad combo for a Dream Merchant or a HowBoy. Branson is a master of this – with his reputation of being a school kid playing on the streets while the curtains of his house remain closed. It is very difficult to analyse Virgin objectively – which leaves his rivals short of weapons to either compete with him or copy him. It also enables him to strike quickly in new markets, with new ideas and surprise tactics.

Strangely enough, Luciano Benetton, although having a vastly different public profile than Branson is much the same. This is a guy who has personally overseen the growth of one of the most powerful brands in the world, a brand bearing his name, but who is hardly known. If I gave anybody reading this book a year and three research assistants, I doubt if you could detail the full, complex corporate architecture of the Benetton family business by the end of it. The public isn't usually aware of what he's doing until after he's done it. Surprise can be a great weapon.

Being unpredictable can work on a number of levels. Again, it can work to your advantage both as you look externally to your 'market' and internally to your own workplace. Remember the old Scot who refused to 'appraise' a quarter of me during an annual review because it was a mystery to him, me and everybody else? Well, I used that quarter a lot. It gained me a reputation, and that got me audiences and resources that I wouldn't normally have secured – people just got intrigued. It also enabled me to recruit people that may otherwise have stayed away – because there is an attraction for some folk in being associated with guys who were raised on a different sort of corporate Jesus. After a while, being unpredictable starts to become the norm, and it can work to your advantage. After all, if you and your team can approach challenges with a mindset that disregards the predictable, then you might find benefits. I figure that if you don't know what you are going to do next, your competition surely can't.

8 *Manage adversity.* Not one of the successes recorded in this book was achieved without setbacks on the way. If the AOL success story was a boxing match, Steve Case eventually won the world championship on points after being on his arse in every round, with the counts against him hovering around the nine mark. Steve Jobs would have been technically declared 'corporately dead' had he been delivered to a hospital in the early 1990s. James Dyson's business fuel tanks were on empty for about eighty percent of his fifteen-year journey.

It is no good hoping you will have an adversity-free run in delivering your project to the world. You won't. If it is to be of any quality, there seems to be a correlation – the greater the Dream, the more ambushes you experience getting there. If the experience of the folk in this book is anything to go by, however, they need not be life-threatening. Indeed, if you look at some of the examples (New Coke?), they are almost a *necessary* pre-requisite of a great Dream. So, they will come. Nobody enjoys them, certainly while they last – but don't fear them. The key is to plan for them, and *plan to manage them.*

When I say 'manage' them, I do not mean you can forecast the details and have a contingency game plan designed in advance for any adversity that might come up. You can for some, but it's the surprise buggers that do the damage – and when I talk about managing them, it is simply about applying a formula to respond to any adversity in a way that minimises the damage and maximises any potential positives that may be hidden in there. The minute you get that sinking feeling, and you know you've been hit, you should go through six quite clear stages of response, i.e:

- Do what is necessary to stabilise the boat. Obviously this depends on where and how you have been hit, and how badly – but nothing else matters in the first responsive stage other than staying afloat. This might be life-or-death stuff, and this is where start-up entrepreneurs are at their best – they do whatever it takes to keep the dream alive. Not growing or prospering, just alive. Beg, borrow, steal, cheat, fight, spit, snarl, eat babies. Whatever. Just stabilise.

- When you have stabilised, VENT. You might be pissed off, frustrated, scared, angry or any combination thereof. Those that the Gods wish to destroy, they first make angry – so get through this stage as fast as you can. But it is important you do it. If you are a screamer, find someplace quiet and SCREAM. If you kick animals, that's OK by me on this occasion, as long as it's not a dog. Do whatever you have to do to depressurise yourself, and cleanse your judgement. Only then can you start putting pieces back together.

- Do not blame anybody but yourself. However unjust, however indirect the causes of the adversity might be, it will not help your resurrection if you blame anybody but yourself. Blaming others may be an absolutely correct allocation of responsibility for the factors involved in the *débacle*, but it just leaves open loops. If it has happened once, it can happen again. You didn't see it coming first time – and that, at this stage is all that matters as far as blame goes. Forget blame, it's useless. Move on.

- Learn what you can. This may be a simple process – i.e. that you avoid repeating the error or the circumstances – but take your time over it. There may be some jewels hidden in what went wrong that, if you mine them, might make for a stronger project. Track what went wrong, right to the root causes. I cannot think of a single project – major or minor – that would not be more robust as a result of this stage being done properly.

- Now, you are ready. Take your first steps forward again. It might be back on the same track, it might be on an entirely different track. But this is where you restart your forward momentum. You might reach this state after a few hours, or it might be months – and that will be a period of frustration. But don't start walking forward again until you are surefooted.

- Last, but not least – get ready, mentally, for the next one. Keep a card with these six stages written on it in your wallet.

Managing adversity is not an art, it is a science. Every one of the famous names in this book overcame adversity on several occasions, and every Dream was stronger for that, and the style of every HowBoy benefited. This can work for you, and it is easy to steal.

9 *Create impact.* By the early 1990s Coca-Cola had recovered its fumble against Pepsi, and had re-established its dominance in most of the battlegrounds where they went head to head. It was time for a knee in the groin. I guess the options were the eastern European theatre, Australasia or the 'home turf' of America. Goizueta chose none of these, but went for Venezuela – in a coup designed to have the most impact, not just on sales of the two rivals, but on Wall Street, the morale of Pepsi people around the world and on their new leader, Roger Enrico. It was a masterstroke by Goizueta, and one that he invested in personally and heavily. Neither side can mortally wound the other, but this move was timed and designed for maximum Impact. It hit centre bull.

Having a winning idea is only part of the battle. Actually getting it on to the launching pad is obviously crucial, but still only part of the challenge. It is no good doing all that good stuff, and then keeping it as a secret – you need to generate *awareness* of what you have which, in turn, will encourage people to try it. Again, as we have seen frequently as we have cherry-picked what has worked for these successful folk, sometimes these activities need to be pointed internally, within the business, as well as externally towards markets and audiences.

All of the folk in the book *created impact*, and no two of them did it the same way. We opened with Benetton's controversial advertising. Roddick pursued her high-profile causes. Jobs masterminded *1984*. Kelleher acted the goat in public and crewed his airplanes with cheerleaders. Branson still spends half his life abseiling down female cleavages that could accommodate my golden retriever. Bollocks to 'location, location, location' – with these folk it was 'impact, impact, impact'.

It is essential to create impact, and it is not very hard to do – and can be quite cost effective. I suggest that if you have a project to develop and launch a green widget, you could create a powerful amount of awareness of it by attaching one to your genitals, and climbing Nelson's Column with no clothes on – having appropriately advised the media in advance, and retained a reasonably efficient PR agency. You would probably sell a few widgets, but I believe the potential downside might weigh heavily against any sales success. I'm thinking here of frostbite, sutures on your whatsit and jail, in that order.

The problem about creating impact is that, as we have seen, the consuming public is nearly deaf and blind to anything you do – simply because there are so many people trying to create their own impact for their own products or services. Some may boringly just spend zillions on adverts that have all the impact of wallpaper – but which get repeated endlessly. Some may go for the single, high-profile event. Some go for a mixture, or both. But to get impact, you have to seize a part of the consuming public's memory, and to do that you must rise way above the street noise. That generally means risking the alienation of some in an attempt to get positively remembered by others. Because if you take a point of view, or get in people's faces, it is a rule of the universe that some will like it, some won't.

This gives us the lesson we must learn about creating impact – that there must be *no person who has NO opinion about what you do*. Our actions must hook people's emotions, and we must recognise that, because of the extreme nature of what we have done to achieve that, then some will love what we offer, others will hate it. And both may be called to action – the lovers to buy the product, the haters to try and stop it. Creating impact is the science of reaching and affecting everybody in a way that, at one end of the spectrum, the 'lovers' will change behaviour – so you try and maximise that. At the other end, the haters will try and stop it – so you try and minimise that.

The lesson we can learn is that the launch of your project is like standing in front of a pond. Forget the little pebbles – go find a big brick and pick the target spot in the water that will create the biggest waves when the brick hits *without coming back over your own shoes*. At least, not too much. Then heave it in.

10 *Lighten up, and have faith in some folk.* I've left these two until last, not only within the chapter, but also within the whole book. The reason for giving them such a place of honour is that – although they are the hardest to see – potentially I believe them to be the most powerful. They have something else in common. If you can use them, they will cost you nothing, and you can start tomorrow.

About a decade or so ago, there was a sort of mini-fashion with a series of *trompe l'oeil* pictures. You know the ones – if you just looked at them as you would a picture in a magazine, they were just a meaningless kaleidoscopic mosaic of colours and shapes. If, however (apparently), you stood (I think) fifteen inches away and stared at them till your groin ached, a clear and beautiful picture would make itself obvious within the chaos. I say 'apparently' because, however correctly I positioned myself, and however hard I stared, nothing ever appeared for me.

I have a feeling that this last section may prove to be the same for some of you. However many times you read the words, you won't see the message. You won't accept the lesson. You won't recognise the conclusion that I'm drawing here from the analyses I made in the book. So, let's take them one at a time, and go slowly.

In the preface to this book, I made the point that business has become grey and miserable. One of the reasons I started to look a bit deeper at the particular folk in this book was that they were anti-grey. Either their style, or achievements, or both, lifted them out of the grey background and made them multicoloured. However, for me to then do the study, and then seem to draw the conclusion that they are all light-hearted comedians, clowning their way to stardom, and that we should try and do the same, is a bit far-fetched. I think I hear you say. You might point a finger at me and tell me that only Herb Kelleher, one out of twelve, would justify this as a conclusion. I would agree – if that were the conclusion I was drawing by calling part of this section: *Lighten Up*.

About thirty years ago, in a second-hand bookstore, I came across a paperback collection of Brendan Behan's early columns for the Irish press. They were his first published works – written between 1954 and 1956, just prior to *The Quare Fellow*. I must have read them about a thousand times. Every time I do I get a spiritual lift. What comes through his writing – which eventually brought him his tragically short but extensive success – was that *he enjoyed it*. My boyhood soccer idol was Denis Law, despite the fact that he left my team for our rivals across the city. Why Denis? Because from whistle to whistle he just seemed to be enjoying himself – celebrating his talent with anybody who was watching. They both rubbed off on me. For twenty odd years I loved Big Business. Yup, I yelled and swore a lot, and the God Of Fuses gave me a very short one – but I enjoyed it, and it showed. I had a lot of a strange thing called Fun, and for every (metaphoric) tear of sadness, there were a thousand tears of laughter. When I stopped smiling, I suddenly realised it was time to go.

Now then. Go back and look at the names in the book. You will find that there is actually only one who *doesn't* give evidence that they enjoyed the journey. Sure, there were setbacks, tensions and tempers for most of them – but the overwhelming message is that what they were doing invigorated and uplifted them. The only exception is Schrempp, and I'm not sure that's valid. Christ only knows what makes him smile now that Poland isn't up for invasion anymore, but even he might have crept one or two in.

So, there is a valid message, and one that we can steal. You will not be a successful Dream Merchant, or HowBoy, unless you enjoy what you do. Period, end of debate. So, lighten up. Celebrate the victories and laugh at the idiocies all around you. Let the world know – or at least those in it who are close to you – that you are having the time of your life. Laugh loudly. It can have an *amazing* effect on the success of what you (and your team) do, and it makes for more blue skies than grey in your corporate life. Everything seems to become that bit easier.

So, on to the last one up – the need to *trust some folk*. On the whole, western industry is crap at trusting anybody unless it absolutely, ABSOLUTELY, has to. The three deadly 'Ps' of modern business life (pressure, pace and paranoia) make it hard to let anything go. If decisions affect you, you want to take 'em. You simply can't risk somebody making mistakes that might come back to bite you in the groin. It's actually easier to do the thing yourself, so that at least you know it's been done properly. Yup, if you are going to build that Dream of yours, you are going to have to do it solo.

Now, if you don't recognise the attitude just summarised as widespread, you are not on the same business planet as the rest of us. And it is a barrelful of Imperial Bollocks. Worse than that, it is the AIDS of modern business life – an evil, growing disease that is difficult to treat.

When I faced the initial challenges of a dead-in-the-water Burger King, to slightly misquote Wodehouse, I might not have been undaunted, but I wasn't very daunted. I got a piece of advice from somebody with many more miles on the clock than me – which was to put two or three 'Centurions' immediately in my team. A Centurion, by his definition, was somebody who had worked with me before, who I knew, and I knew I could rely on to do a specific job. The second part of the advice was *to then leave them alone*, and for me to concentrate my efforts on the other parts of the business – which had been run, I believe, by aliens. It was a magic formula – none of us could have made it work any other way.

Centurion, in its old Roman meaning, is a good descriptive word for these people. Hold on to it, and scan back through the book. Benetton's siblings; Branson's kitchen cabinet; Dell's Office of the Chairman; Roy Disney; Gordon Roddick; Donald Keogh of Coca-Cola and *thousands* of people in Southwest Airlines and Starbucks. They are all Centurions. They are not the people who will be remembered as the Dream Merchants, or as the HowBoy legends, but they are the people without whom the triumphs would have been qualified, reduced or non-existent. In almost all the examples, at some stage, and in some cases at many stages, the 'legends' put their Dreams in the hands of their Centurions, and had faith. The results are in the History Book of Business for all to see.

– oooOOOooo –

We are at the end. If you've been with me all the way, I thank you for your perseverance. I hope you've learned a few bits and pieces about all these folk on the way. In addition, it is impossible for me to take on something like this without having a laugh or two – and I hope you have managed to join in now and again. I finished by identifying ten things you could steal from these folk, some of which might help you realise your Dream – whatever its size and stature. Some of the other 'lessons' might help you become a better HowBoy or Howgirl – enabling the *way* you do business to be more rewarding for you and your company.

I hope it works for you – spectacularly. Then, I hope others are influenced by you, and others, in turn by them. It's not that I want you all to become rich and famous, although I have nothing against mass wealth creation in general and for you in particular. No, my goals here are not about success or money – they are about changing colour. The folk in this book did their part to bring colour to a greying business world. Today, despite their efforts, it is now virtually all grey. It's not even a warming, welcoming autumn sort of grey – it's the grey you get when it's pissing down with rain and it's set in for the day.

So, basically, you – yes, YOU – are the only hope for Planet Business. Go back to your workplace, and start to add a dab of colour here and there. And you, in turn, must spread the word – so buy as many copies of this book as you need for your subordinates, peers and your boss. *Particularly* your boss.

You all paint, and I'll get rich. How's *that* for a deal?

nutter talk:

These you can steal:

1 Milk your influences
2 Fuse different elements together
3 Take a restless pill
4 Control what you must
5 Do not masturbate
6 Pick your challenge
7 Wrap your riddle in a mystery and then in an enigma
8 Manage adversity
9 Create impact
10 Lighten up and have faith in some folk

SOURCES AND FURTHER READING

FIRST AND FOREMOST, this is not an official or authorised biography of any of the business icons covered in this book. They are
not meant to be fully researched and/or original biographies
– in almost all cases these have been done by others.

In addition, I have not sent any of those still living final drafts
for either permission or forgiveness. Here's my logic – none of these
folk, to my knowledge, have asked my permission to write a book
about me. So there.

I am not an academic, and this book is not an academic study. I
am the least guru-esque person you know. But I am an avid reader,
watcher and digester of information. I spent a large chunk of the
last decade on commercial airlines, almost always accompanied by a
double handful of magazines, journals and books. I rarely emerged

without bits of paper sticking out of assorted pockets, with (what proved to be later) illegible scribble on them (along with the odd red wine stain).

I have, therefore, only a hazy idea about the genesis of many of my ideas in this work, but most of them are from the following general and specific sources. Add to them the subscriber's Web sites for *Business Week* and *The Economist*. Certainly, where I have used a specific quote or reference, the source will be included below.

Company Man: The Rise And Fall of Corporate Life, Anthony Sampson, HarperCollins, 1995.

The World According to Peter Drucker, Jack Beatty, Simon & Schuster, 1998.

The Wealth and Poverty of Nations, David Landes, Norton, 1998.

Harvard Business Review, Business Classics, HBS Publishing, 1991.

Beyond Certainty, Charles Handy, Hutchinson, 1995.

Up the Organisation, Robert Townshend, Michael Joseph, 1970.

The Ultimate Business Library, Stuart Crainer, Capstone, 1998.

New Ideas From Dead Economists, Todd Buchholz, Penguin, 1990.

Ready, Blame, Fire, Ira Blumenthal, Griffin, 1998.

The State We're In, Will Hutton, Vintage, 1995.

The Prince, Nicolo Machievelli, Wordsworth Edition, 1997.

Built To Last: Successful Habits of Visionary Companies, James Collins and Jerry Porras, HarperBusiness, 1994.

Brand Warriors, edited by Fiona Gilmore, HarperCollins Business,

Ultimate Business Breakthroughs, Tom Cannon, Capstone, 2000.

The March of Folly, Barbara Tuchman, Ballantine, 1984.

Forbes: The Greatest Business Stories of All Time, Daniel Goss, Wiley, 1996.

No Logo, Naomi Klein, Flamingo/HarperCollins, 2001.

Benetton: The Family, the Business and the Brand, Jonathan Mantle, Warner, 1999.

An Autobiography, James Dyson (and Giles Coren), Nixon Business, 1997.

Direct From Dell, Michael Dell, HarperCollins, 1999.

Business the Dell Way, Rebecca Saunders, Capstone, 2000.

Business As Unusual, Anita Roddick, Thorsons, 2000.

I'd Like to Buy the World a Coke: The Life and Times of Roberto Goizuetta, D. Griesling, Wiley, 1997.

For God, Country and Coca-Cola, M. Prendergast, Phoenix, 1993.

The Real Walt Disney, L. Mosely, Grafton, 1997.

Building a Company – Roy Disney and the Creation of an Entertainment Empire, Bob Thomas, Hyperion, 1998.

Virgin King, Tom Jackson, HarperCollins, 1995.

Business the Richard Branson Way, D. Dearlove, AMACOM, 1999.

Richard Branson – An Authorised Biography, M. Brown, Headline, 1998.

Apple Confidential, Owen Linzmayer, Publishers Group, 1999.

On the Firing Line. Gil Amelio (and W. Simon), HarperCollins, 1998.

Odyssey – Pepsi to Apple, John Sculley (and J. Byrne), Harper & Row, 1987.

The Second Coming of Steve Jobs, Alan Deuthschman, Broadway Books, 2000.

Nuts – Southwest Airlines' Crazy Recipe for Business and Personal Success, K and J Freiburg, Bard Press, 1996.

Jürgen Schrempp and the Making of an Auto Dynasty, Jürgen Grässlin, McGraw Hill, 1998.

AOL.com, Kari Swisher, Times Books/Random House, 1998.

Pour Your Heart in It, Howard Schultz and Dori Jones Young, Hyperion, 1998.

INDEX